GREEN CLEANING

ECO-FRIENDLY TIPS & TRICKS

ALISA & CYNTHIA MAYNE

 First published 2021 by Wilkinson Publishing Pty Ltd
ACN 006 042 173
Wilkinson Publishing
PO Box 24135, Melbourne, VIC 3001, Australia
Ph: +61 3 9654 5446
www.wilkinsonpublishing.com.au

Cover and book design by Tango Media.
Printed and bound in Australia by Griffin Press, part of Ovato.

ISBN: 9781925927443

A catalogue record for this book is available from the National Library of Australia.

Follow Wilkinson Publishing on social media and let us know
how your green cleaning goes.

f WilkinsonPublishing

⊙ wilkinsonpublishinghouse

🐦 WPBooks

This book was co-written by and dedicated to my wonderful Mumma, Cynthia Mayne. Mumma, together we wrote books based on what you taught us, to help people realise that life is wonderful no matter what your budget, and your wise words have helped so many. Everything I have learnt I learnt from you. Your unconditional love and compassion were truly unique. Your cheeky enthusiasm for life was infectious and your never-ending quest to help people was inspiring. You gave so much and lived life to the absolute fullest.

There will never be another like you and you are sorely missed by us all. Rest in Peace beautiful Mumma, we are so proud of you. Xxoo

Metric Conversion

For some of our readers, it might be helpful to refer to the following charts in order to covert the recipes in this book from metric measurements to standard (or customary) units, which are typically used in the United States.

Please note that metric 'cup and spoon' measurements are only slightly larger than standard measurements, so they can be used virtually interchangeably with the metric measurements listed in the recipes. Often, you will find that both metric and standard measurements appear on liquid and dry measuring utensils.

Liquid and Dry Measure Equivalencies *	
CUSTOMARY	**METRIC**
¼ teaspoon	1.25 ml
½ teaspoon	2.5 ml
1 teaspoon	5 ml
1 tablespoon	15 ml
1 fluid ounce	30ml
¼ cup	60ml
⅓ cup	80ml
½ cup	120ml
1 cup	240ml
1 pint (2 cups)	480ml
1 quart (4 cups)	960ml
1 gallon	3.84 litres

1 quart = 32 ounces = *approximately* 1 litre (0.96 litres)

By weight	
1 ounce	28 grams
¼ pound	114 grams
1 pound	454 grams (0.45 kilograms)
2.2 pounds	1 kilogram (1,000 grams)

Oven Temperature Equivalencies *		
DESCRIPTION	**°F**	**°C**
Cool	200	90
Very Low	250	120
Low	300-325	150-160
Medium Low	325-350	160-180
Medium	350-375	180-190
Medium High	375-400	190-200
Hot	400-450	200-230
Very Hot	450-500	230-260

*All equivalencies are approximate and are provided by the United States National Institute of Standards and Technology (NIST), US Department of Commerce.

Converting from Metric Units to US Customary Units **

WHEN YOU KNOW	MULTIPLY BY	TO FIND
Mass		
grams (g)	0.035	ounces (oz)
kilograms (kg)	2.2	pounds (lb)
Volume		
millilitres (ml)	0.03	fluid ounces (fl oz)
litres (L)	2.1	pints (pt)
litres (L)	1.06	quarts (qt)
litres (L)	0.26	gallons (gal)
Temperature (exact conversion)		
°C (degrees Celsius)	multiply by 9/5, add 32	°F (degrees Fahrenheit)

Converting from US Customary Units to Metric Units **

WHEN YOU KNOW	MULTIPLY BY	TO FIND
Mass		
ounces (oz)	28	grams (g)
pounds (lb)	0.45	kilograms (kg)
Volume		
fluid ounces (fl oz)	30	millilitres (ml)
pints (pt)	0.47	litres (L)
quarts (qt)	0.95	litres (L)
gallons (gal)	3.8	litres (L)
Temperature (exact conversion)		
°F (degrees Fahrenheit)	subtract 32, multiply by 5/9	°C (degrees Celsius)

**All conversions are approximate except for Temperature, which is exact.

CONTENTS

INTRODUCTION

The year 2020 was certainly one we will all never forget!

Never before have we all had so much time in our homes and never before has the need for health and hygiene been so important. COVID-19 certainly gave us all a new appreciation for our cozy (and sometimes not-so-cozy houses) over the interesting and ever-changing times. For many of us it also gave us a new and exciting opportunity to spend more time in the place that we all cherish (our homes) and for many of us it highlighted the need for a clean and healthy home environment. Germs and bacteria are always around us but there is no need to fill your home with an overload of toxic chemicals to eradicate them.

If we have all learnt one universal lesson from COVID-19 it was 'wash your hands in soap and water'. Yes, hand sanitizer and disinfectant also do the same job (and in times of emergency are needed) but for most of us all we need to do is the simple act of washing your hands in soap and water for 20 seconds to attain the same results (minus the chemicals). This is such a wonderful way to remind ourselves that having a healthy home and keeping our selves healthy can be done in a non-toxic way.

In this new edition of our bestselling natural cleaning book, we can help you enjoy having a home free of chemicals and still free of germs! (And let's not forget free of single use plastics and free of waste that the planet and we all, need to stay focused on.)

I am excited to share lots of new ideas and handy home hints along with our original fun and useful cleaning tips that can fil your home with fresh, safe, healthy and easy ways to keep germs at bay and your home sparkling and clean in every room.

Packaging targeting the fear of germs will be in overload in our supermarkets for the near future and it shouldn't have to be a scary onslaught when you enter the shops.

If we all stick to the basics and use a safe and healthy approach to simple hygiene and embrace the changing times (instead of being fearful of them) we can save on our shopping bills, enjoy a clean home, consume less waste, save time shopping and help the planet and our waterways by being mindful of what we use and how we use it. You may even find that you enjoy this new simple way of life and with the time and money saved you can share them with your friends and family as gifts!

Sometimes some of the simplest options cost nothing at all! And take zero time! But achieve amazing results (something the big brand cleaning companies are not keen on us finding out about).

For example, did you know that sunlight is a natural sanitizer that far outweighs most commercial cleaning products! Simply laying your pillows or sheets in the hot sunlight can remove a host of bacteria and germs and will also whiten your sheets better than any store-bought sheet whitener. Not only is this free but it's also quick, uses no packaging and creates no waste. The Sun's ability to clean, disinfect, sanitise and kill harmful bacteria as well as bleach is quite mind blowing and so simple! Who doesn't love the smell of fresh sheets straight from the line? And did you ever wonder how your granny got her sheets and clothes so fresh and white? Chances are it was the Sun doing a lot of the work.

Similarly, air quality products are a massive market, promoting clean air in your home is very important, but you don't need to buy electric gadgets that need power and energy and money to clean your home. Simply opening all the doors and windows of your home and allowing the sunshine and fresh air in once a day and flushing out the stale air will give you very similar results (and you don't have to pay the power bill at the end).

Pulling your sheets back each morning instead of making your bed can refresh the air flow, stop bugs and mites breeding and give your bed a longer life span (and save you time making your bed!).

So as the cleaning companies amp up their marketing campaigns let us all enjoy taking a moment and re-evaluating what we actually want in our homes and our landfill!

Let's all remember that washing your hands regularly with soap was what the world health organization recommended. Let us all remember that bringing more toxic chemicals into our homes is not a solution but actually a gimmick to make us consumer more.

We can all enjoy clean homes and enjoy them clean from chemicals too! It's simple, it's easy and sometimes it's even fun!

Since we first released this book eight years ago, we have received so many wonderful emails and updates on your cleaning and clean home journey. It's been an endless joy hearing about your delight in having a clean and chemical free home. I am so excited to continue sharing ideas and to continue hearing about how much they have helped you.

The world has changed quite a bit since 2010 when we first started writing this book and over the last four reprints, we have had so much fun adding to each addition.

This edition will be updated without my beloved Mum, but her wisdom, advice and timeless skills will still be here. They are simply too good not to share. Her years of raising us being fully self-sufficient had a massive impact on me as a child and the valuable lessons I learnt from a simple and peaceful home have been bound to me for life.

Such little things as not having a cleaning cupboard packed with spray bottles and chemicals or highly scented cleaning agents was just something we were used to. But for too many people the cleaning aisle is one that can fill half a shopping cart! But the reality is that the outcome of both options was a clean home (ours was just free of the toxic chemicals, plastics and complicated application directions). I know that many would love to have a home that smells of fresh lemon rather than bleach and a shopping trip that avoided the cleaning aisle altogether.

Taking charge of what you put in your shopping trolley is such a wonderful and powerful way to take hold of your life, health and bank account. It's exciting to know that you can acquire the same results as the adverts on TV will lead you to believe BY NOT purchasing that product and instead making your own.

With the world moving at a pace that most of us race to catch with, now more than ever we have the power to press the pause button and reset how we will restart what we bring into our home.

A simple life is a lovely life and the fabulous side effects of this lifestyle is more money, less chemicals, a happier planet, more time, less waste and less toxins for your body to have to process.

There is currently a huge rise of hormone imbalances and research shows that a large percentage of these are from giving our bodies too many outside chemicals to process. There has never been a better time to start the journey of a clean home, clean from germs, clean from chemicals and just sparking clean! And I can't wait to share them all with you.

This book was written as a workbook, you can start your new cleaning journey by simply embracing one new way to clean at the start, or by using many of the tips at once. Each tiny change makes a big change over time. Each chemical cleaning product that you leave on the supermarket shelf and instead make yourself, is an inspiring step towards a simple, clean, healthy and happy home.

WE WERE LUCKY

We were lucky to grow up self-sufficiently in a little cottage in the Victorian mountains.

Mum and Dad chose to be completely self-sufficient for most of our younger years, they took the leap and committed themselves to the self-sufficient lifestyle fully—like many others in the '70s—and it is a choice I am eternally grateful for. Our youth was spent gardening, making soap, baking bread, cooking, collecting eggs, helping milk the cows and generally living a very peaceful existence.

Life had a slow pace and we learnt to be grateful for everything in our home, as we had made it with our own hands! We also got to spend lots of time with our parents, helping them and learning heaps along the way. We learnt to be capable and responsible at a very early age, lots of jobs needed to be done (it is a not an easy lifestyle!) but we have so many wonderful memoires because of it: hunting for mushrooms, catching slugs, collecting apples, sleeping in wheelbarrow when the days were long, and chasing chickens, or in my case, cuddling chickens and reading them *The Magic Faraway Tree* in a tree!

I may not have the intense commitment as Mum and Dad to be fully self-sufficient, but I have kept a lot of those peaceful ways, integrated them into my modern life and still do to this day!

One of my all-time favourite practices I continue is eating dinner by candlelight.

As kids we lived without the constant sound of electrical buzzing of refrigerators, TVs or anything that is plugged in. I have never forgotten the peacefulness and calmness that comes with the lack of that never-ending buzzing in the background. So, when life is getting too busy and we are feeling a little frazzled, we turn everything off (even the fridge sometimes) and just sit quietly, chat and have our dinner by candlelight. It is absolutely beautiful and such a lovely way to refuel after a long day.

It is so wonderful that people around the world are doing Earth Hour each year, but you don't need to wait for a special time, you can do it every single night in your home. Not only does it save electricity—which helps the planet and your wallet—but it just recharges your whole body, helps you sleep better, gives you that connection with your family that we all strive for and helps you sleep so much better! there is something so serene about the candlelight, the light is gentle on your eyes and the lack of the buzzing electrical background noise gives your mind a chance to refresh. If you haven't tried it, give it a go! We did it every night for a year and when friends would come over for dinner, they loved it too! In fact, no-one wanted to turn the lights on afterwards. Such a simple trick but imagine how much power we could all save as a collective if we all had an hour of no power each night! And it is as easy as flicking off a switch and lighting a candle, I guarantee you will be amazed at how refreshing it is!

● ● ●

Another thing growing up self-sufficiently taught me is to appreciate that time and energy put in creates a much better feeling of satisfaction at the end!

Over the decades, companies have spent billions on advertising trying to convince us all that convenience is the reward! This may be all well and good, but if you do not plan to spend that saved time on anything else rewarding then you have not really gained anything at all. If that time saved is spent watching more advertising trying to sell you more products that is time wasted (not for the advertising companies).

Making your own cleaning products or growing your own plants and vegetables takes time, there is no denying that. But absolutely nothing bought from a big corporation can ever give you the immense satisfaction of making your own! I really believe that it is one of the big life lessons that is slowly being sold out from under us.

As most people know, turning off the TV and teaching yourself something new has benefits well beyond saving a few dollars and helping the planet. The best part is that you can never stop learning new things! It becomes addictive and before you know it, the TV is never on (or in our case we just do not have one anymore!) and you have a craving to learn more, create more, add more skills to your collection and therefore be more capable and feel better about yourself!

Life was not meant to be all about having endless free time, it was meant to be filled with projects and tasks and work and friends and families. This false dream that marketing companies sell—that convenience equals happiness—is stripping people of learning skills and experiencing all the joy and frustration and problem-solving skills that go with learning new things! Not to mention that this 'convenience' is literally filling our planet with waste that will take hundreds of years to break down, destroying our waterways and killing our wildlife along the way. All to save a little time! Time is something we all have an equal amount of—rich and poor, we all have exactly the same amount of it each day! If we can all choose to use a little of that to make and create, we can really have a phenomenal impact on the planet, and it comes with a healthy side dose of satisfaction.

● ● ●

I was so lucky to have a mum that was kind and caring but also never stopped striving to give, to learn and to share. No idea we had as kids was too crazy and her attitude was always 'Go for it! You never know until you give it a go!' There was also never any failure because trying was the goal! If you succeeded, then that was just a bonus.

Because of this, us kids have all tried MANY different careers and had a huge array of varied jobs and businesses along the way, learnt more than we ever could have dreamed and plan to learn lots more. Always with the support of Mum and Dad, and because the goal was always about giving it a go, we always had lots of laughs and were never too hard on ourselves if it didn't work out the way we had planned. If there is anything that I would love to share the most from this book, that is it!

We lost our beloved Mumma eight years ago, her passing was a huge blow to us a family but we all knew that there was nothing she wanted more than for us all to keep on going and learning and sharing and creating. Mum and I wrote this book not long before she passed and its shared a lot of tips and hopefully helped a lot of people through its manly reprints. As the years have passed, the world has changed and is still changing, for the better! I wish she was here to see how many people appreciate simple living and caring for our planet. But nothing ever happens if you don't give it a go!

Together—one little green cleaner at a time—we call all create such a wonderful change that goes beyond what we may even believe, because if you just give it a go, and you share your tips with friends and they go on to learn and in turn share also, we can make a quiet little ripple of change that will continue long after we have all passed. It all starts somewhere and it starts when we all just give it a go! So don't be shy and never worry if perhaps things don't work out exactly as you planned—the fact that we all want to do something is the big something that's the goal!

Always be excited to try and to share and to learn as you go, every step is a step in the right direction. Feel free to tweak any of the tips in this book if you feel they suit you better that way and pass them on to friends and family. Together we can all quietly make a greener planet.

THE SECRETS BIG COMPANIES DON'T WANT YOU TO KNOW

Although cleaning products aren't a major part of the household budget, they are expensive and the cost of creams, polishes, powders and spray-on cleaners can be replaced with simple homemade products that work just as well for a fraction of the cost.

The aisle for cleaning products is interesting to say the least—the variety is enormous and the scents overwhelming. There are so many things to do 'this' and 'that' to anything around your house it's hard to imagine that all we need to clean our homes is a few simple ingredients that can be bought in bulk for very little outlay.

Companies use the same base formula for many products. We know this because we used to supply a major supermarket with a range of cleaners. Don't be fooled by the array of products on sale, most have the same active ingredient and often all that changes is the perfume, colouring and the ratio of active ingredient to water.

A base formula for a kitchen counter spray is often the same as an engine degreaser, they are just mixed in different ratios then presented in eye catching packaging giving the subtle message that we need to buy different products for each job. There's nothing wrong with these marketing games, after all 'that's business'. Cash in on the secrets of the big companies and make your home the centre for the business of saving money, reducing landfill and protecting our precious environment.

SIMPLE CHANGES

They say change is not easy, especially in a world where time is short and stress levels high. Habit keeps us in a rut where we can be tempted to reach out for familiar items without giving thought to what we are really doing. Because change can be hard, especially in a busy household, try leaving notes around the house to avoid falling into old habits. Eventually new habits form and the notes can be discarded. In the marketing and business world this is called the 6 x 4 system—messages on cards 6" x 4" as constant reminders of what we need to do.

To make the transition from consumerism to homemade products stress free, put aside a place to store your basic ingredients—somewhere easy to get to. Then set about changing labels on the cleaning products you already have. The trick is to make the transition process as easy as possible and then you won't fall back into old habits.

Work with the principle of *waste not want not* and finish the commercial products you already have in your cupboard. Cover the commercial labels with your home formulae label and when the bottle is empty you're ready to move into action.

If you're lucky enough to still have the pitter-patter of tiny (or not so tiny) feet around the house, ask the kids to liven the labels up with drawings and bright colours. Maybe they would like to choose names for each product. Getting them involved is a great way to help them understand the subtle methods of marketing because nothing teaches more than 'doing'.

You can be guaranteed that involving children in any activity will be more effective than any 6 x 4 reminder card system and it won't be long before your cupboards will outshine any supermarket aisle for colour and vibrancy.

PREPARE AHEAD OF TIME

When you prepare your mixture ahead of time it does make it easier to avoid being tempted to reach for that quick fix—the commercial alternative—and because, like commercial products, our homemade products will often have the same common active ingredients, it's a logical step to make bulk batches, store, then dilute as needed.

Being prepared also saves you the bother of having to remember all the various uses and formulations in your head. Label the container according to the purpose, include the formula for easy refilling and your work is done.

Squeeze-top and spray-nozzle plastic bottles make good containers for liquids; a big plastic salt shaker with large holes in the top makes a good container for powders, and wide mouthed plastic containers with a screw lids are ideal for gumption or paste cleaners.

It won't be long before commercial products are well and truly a thing of the past.

IT MAKES SENSE
AND CENTS

Some ingredients are best purchased in bulk, which means you'll have enough raw ingredients to last a very long time. This isn't necessarily a bad thing because the ingredients won't go off if stored properly and buying in bulk offers another possibility—a source of some money on the side. Round up a few busy friends and sell them your surplus at a minimal cost. Bartering with products in a suburban situation may not be convenient but bartering with money, the most common transaction is fail-proof and here is where your surplus product can make you extra cash, saving your friends money at the same time.

We know people find it hard to imagine cleaning the kitchen counter for one cent or making an all-purpose spray cleaner for three cents, but that's about all the raw ingredients in those highly priced products on the supermarket shelves cost the manufacturer. The rest is all in marketing, labelling, packaging, freight and presentation.

Now that you are becoming your own marketing company, labelling and packaging company, freight carrier and retailer, you're first in line to pick up the savings.

If you're keen on delicate perfumes and essential oils we encourage you to experiment. You may even come up with something totally new.

A word of warning before you get started on your own recipes – some combinations can be toxic. Avoid mixing ammonia and bicarb soda; this mixture releases toxic gas (it's always advisable to avoid inhaling ammonia under any circumstances).

INTRODUCING OTHERS TO NATURAL PRODUCTS

Once the money-saving and effective recipes and tricks in this book have taken hold of you, you might understandably want to preach their word with all the fervour and zeal of a religious convert who has seen the natural cleaning light. Chances are that approach will go over like a lead balloon. Instead, try some more subtle ways to introduce others to the fiscal and environmental benefits of being your own cleaning product factory. Take your cue from the suggestions below and come up with many more on your own! Hopefully your generosity will spark a chain of giving that inspires more people to clean the natural way.

+ **Housewarming/welcome wagon:** If you have a new family in the neighbourhood, or if friends are throwing a housewarming, a basket of natural cleaning products makes for a welcome and useful gift to celebrate their move and will go a long way to help them get situated in their new home, where there will be plenty to clean before they've even lived in it a day.

+ **Raffle prize at a local function:** Raffle tickets are a great way for organisations to raise a little extra money during social functions. If you'd like to donate to the prize pool but are a bit strapped for cash, people will appreciate the time and talent you put into a selection of homemade products like laundry sprays and essential oil atomisers.

✦ **Hostess (or Host) gift:** The Tupperware party has returned in many forms from jewellery and makeup to bags and bins. Side businesses are a great way to make a little extra money when in an economic crunch and offer a wonderful excuse to socialise on a weeknight. If you will be hosting a shopping party, as a token of thanks why not send your guests home with a little 'goodie bottle'—they'll appreciate the gesture of gratitude and hospitality and might become repeat customers.

✦ **Secret Santa:** Does your co-worker or third cousin twice removed really need another novelty mug or hideous holiday sweater? Break the cycle of bad compulsory gift giving next holiday season and instead present them with a tasteful collection of homemade hand creams or room sprays and laundry fresheners. The lucky recipient you drew in the lottery will be knocking on your office door and ringing your phone come January for the recipes.

✦ **Shameless plug:** Place a note card in with your bundle or tie a tag around your atomiser explaining where you obtained the formulas for the products you gift or donate. Or, if you're feeling extra generous, include a copy of *Green Cleaning* in the bundle or as a door prize so that they can benefit from all the formulas in this book.

STOCK YOUR CUPBOARD

You'll save heaps if you buy in bulk from a produce store—you can save up to 80%—and because these ingredients don't expire there's no problem with waste.

+ Pure soap
+ Bicarb soda
+ Sodium per-carbonate
+ Citric acid
+ White vinegar
+ Borax
+ Washing soda
+ Cloudy ammonia
+ Salt (bulk)
+ Tea tree or eucalyptus oil
+ Lemon juice (fresh)

Pure Soap

Pure soap is the best to work with but is not always readily available so look for a good quality laundry soap bar.

I make a bulk mixture of liquid soap from one bar of soap grated and dissolved in 10 litres of water and store it in an old plastic water container with a tap so it's easy to decant. This ratio works for me but experiment with what suits your climate—in a cold climate the mixture will thicken on cold days but if you live in a hot climate you can probably reduce the water and use a more concentrated liquid. Either way you'll find your perfect mix after some experiments.

Grating soap can be a bit of a bore, especially if the bar has been wet or you have wet hands—the soap slips and slides all over the place. If you find grating a chore try cutting the soap into little pieces with a large knife. It will come away in long shards that may take a bit longer to dissolve but is much faster than grating. Make sure you clean the bench and grater or knife as soon as you've finished. Your family won't share your sense of humour if you laugh when they pick up what they think are left over gratings of cheese from the bench to nibble as they pass by!

To make the bulk liquid soap

1. Dissolve 1 bar of grated soap in 2 litres of water in a large pan over medium heat.
2. Let the mixture cool.
3. Pour the dissolved liquid into a 10-litre container (an old water container is perfect) then top with a further eight litres of cold water. This will give you a total of around 10 litres of liquid soap.

Note: If you put the container with the dissolved soap liquid under the tap to top it up you'll find that bubbles will quickly take over. Avoid creating a container full of bubbles by pouring the water in at an angle, as you would pour a beer, or add the water first then top up with the concentrated soap liquid. It's a bit like life—slow and steady is the best pace.

If you don't have an empty 10 litre container use 5 x 2 litre milk containers and use the same ratio: ¼ melted soap to ¾ cold water. The container is not important, as long as it's convenient for you to handle.

The added water keeps the mixture liquid. A strong mixture will solidify when it's cold, which isn't particularly a problem because you can reheat it easily. Adding the extra cold water just saves you the bother.

Bicarbonate of Soda

Grandma's kitchen was never without it.

Chemically known as sodium bicarbonate, it's a soda ash which occurs naturally. It is refined to produce a pure safe product with many uses. It is not a chemical compound.

The beauty of bicarb, as it's commonly referred to, is that it helps regulate pH and balance acidity or alkalinity, which is why it's used a lot in food production. It's a neutraliser—the ultimate mediator with no end of uses including detergents, soakers, hair products and as an odour absorber. It's even used to make our bread rise.

The bicarb soda you use in your fridge, freezer or cupboard to eliminate odours can be used to clean your counters, floors and in your laundry. It's also a superb toothpaste and tooth whitener.

If kept for long periods or exposed to moisture it tends to clump, just tap with a wooden spoon to break up any lumps. A simple way of keeping it in easy-flow mode is to store bicarb in the fridge, because refrigerators dry things out.

Bicarb has so many uses we could do a book on that subject alone but all you need to know is that it's very safe for you, your family, your wallet and the environment.

Sodium per-carbonate

Sodium per-carbonate is basically a solid form of hydrogen peroxide and is an environmentally safe whitening agent and deodoriser used in commercial laundry and cleaning products.

It can be obtained from chemical suppliers, pool supply companies and from the internet.

Sodium per-carbonate is not cheap, but it is so powerful that you literally need only a pinch to get the desired boost.

Citric Acid

Citric Acid is a dry powder or crystal and is often called 'sour salt'. It is used extensively in cosmetics, foods and soft drinks, a host of industrial applications and has proven to be an excellent de-greaser and cleaning agent.

Citric binds metals, cleans scale, adds bubbles to soft drinks, holds colour in jams, is used in ice cream as an emulsifying agent and in bath bombs and effervescent tablets—it is a most versatile product.

It is sold in supermarkets in small containers and can also be bought in larger quantities (and cheaper) from the chemist or wholesale distributors.

Vinegar

Or if you're French, 'vinaigre' meaning 'sour wine', which is exactly how it was discovered thousands of years ago from a barrel of wine that had gone bad.

The history of vinegar goes back 10,000 years when it was used by everyone—kings, queens and peasants. It's a testament to the value of vinegar in the lives of our ancestors that it was the only product shared across all classes of society, rich and poor alike.

There are thousands of uses for vinegar to back the claim that vinegar is 'the product that can do anything'.

Getting technical: vinegar is an acidic liquid processed from the fermentation of ethanol in a process that yields acetic acid (ethanoic acid). The concentration ranges from 4% to 8% by volume when it's table vinegar (usually around 5%) and up to 18% for other uses.

Natural vinegars also contain small amounts of tartaric acid, citric acid and other acids and if you're lucky enough to get hold of a table vinegar with the 'mother' you know you've got the best on offer. Vinegar is a live product; the mother is the sediment formed in the processing and appears as a semi solid mass in top quality vinegars—a great internal cleanser.

But back to the household variety of cleanser—white vinegar. It's cheap, easy to use, totally natural and totally safe.

Borax

Borax—or sodium borate as it's also known—is another fantastic natural substance. It was first discovered over 4,000 years ago and is a naturally occurring alkaline mineral.

Borax is usually found in the cleaning aisle of your supermarket (probably on the bottom shelf) and would be near the laundry powders and soaps, but the cheapest way is to buy it in bulk from hardware or produce stores.

The most common use for Borax is as a laundry booster, it is fantastic if you live in an area with hard water because it's a superb water softener and leaves your clothes clean and bright.

Borax has been used for many generations for a range of things from disinfecting and deodorising to preserving cut flowers and even repelling bugs.

It has no toxic fumes and is safe for the environment—but take note that it can irritate the skin and should never be ingested.

Borax is a fantastic cleaning agent and as you will see in the recipes on the pages ahead, the good well outweighs the bad when it comes to borax.

Washing Soda

Not to be confused with washing powder, which is a powdered soap and detergent; washing soda, closely related to baking soda, is a highly alkaline chemical compound that is fantastic as a cleaning agent.

Washing soda is also known as sodium carbonate and is also called soda ash; this is because one of the main sources of washing soda comes from the ash of plants.

As the name infers, washing soda's most common use is in the laundry as the high alkalinity helps it act as a solvent to remove stains.

But its ability goes well beyond the laundry. It doesn't stain like bleach, is a brilliant de-scaler and anything that's hard to clean due to mineral build up will clean in no time with washing soda.

Textile artists use washing soda to help dyes adhere to fabric, which in turn gives the fabric longer lasting colour (colourfast).

Washing soda is a heavy hitting cleaner that is perfect for stoves and any job that has most other cleaning products beat.

A note of warning: washing soda is caustic in large doses, so label it well and keep it out of reach of little hands and pets. Be careful not to inhale it and make sure you wear gloves when handling.

Lemon Juice

Most common commercial cleaning products contain lemon (or a chemically enhanced substitute) because the fresh scent of lemons makes people think of cleanliness, and because the citric acid contained in lemons is a strong cleaning agent. It's also a natural antiseptic.

The best lemons to use are those that have smooth, oily skins and are heavy for their size (meaning plenty of juice). They should be bright yellow (ripe) with no green tinges (not ripe yet). Meyer lemons are the most alkaline and have very little pectin, while Lisbon or Eureka varieties are more acidic with plenty of pectin, which is why they are preferred for jam making.

Lemons keep well at room temperature but keep better in a cool, dry environment, and lemon zest (peel) can be frozen for months.

Depending on where you live lemon trees can be grown fairly easily, if you don't have a tree of your own keep an eye out for a tree in someone else's backyard and come to an arrangement to relieve the owner of the unwanted crop; maybe share your homemade cleaning products with them, or maybe they would just appreciate the surplus fruit being collected rather than rotting on the ground.

To get the most amount of juice the lemon should be at room temperature. Use the palm of your hand to roll the lemon on a hard surface to help improve juice yields.

If you only need a small amount of juice and don't want to waste a whole lemon pierce the end of the lemon with a fork, squeeze out the amount of juice needed, cover the holes with tape and then store in the fridge. Or you could cut a small sliver of rind and when you've taken what juice you need simply replace the rind back over the hole. It will re-seal itself and be ready for next time. Isn't nature great, a no fuss, superbly fashioned, environmentally friendly container at your fingertips!

Lemons are another of nature's magic products that smell good, store well, are environmentally friendly and don't cost the earth.

Lemon Alternatives

Many plants taste or smell similar to lemons and can serve as either flavour or scent substitutes, though they cannot necessarily mimic lemon's cleansing and antiseptic properties.

+ Certain cultivars of basil such as lemon basil (also known as Indonesian basil), Thai lemon basil, and lime basil are used in Asian cooking.
+ Certain cultivars of mint such as lemon balm and lemon mint (also known as purple horsemint) when crushed emit a lemony scent.
+ Lemongrass (Cymbopogon) is a genus of 55 species of grasses native to warm and tropical climates. Lemongrass is commonly used in teas, soups and curries in Asian cuisine. Its oil is sometimes used as a pesticide and preservative as well as a lure for honeybees.
+ Lemon myrtle (or lemon scented ironwood or sweet verbena tree) is native to the subtropical rainforests of Queensland, Australia. It is cultivated for cooking and as an essential oil. The dried leaf has antioxidant properties.
+ Lemon thyme smells and tastes like lemon. Its tiny leaves can be used in any recipes that call for lemons, even marinades.
+ Lemon verbena is a shrub whose leaves emit a lemon scent when bruised and is considered the most strongly scented of the lemon scented plants. It is used as a lemon substitute in cooking and in place of actual lemon in tea infusions. It has strong antioxidant properties.

✦ A note about limes: lemons and limes, both citrus fruits, share some similar properties but are not the same. Limes are green in colour and smaller than lemons. They also have a bittersweet taste to lemon's sour. Limes do not have the same high concentration of vitamin C so they are a weak substitute for lemon's astringent properties but their scent can be a pleasant addition to cleaning products.

Salt

Salt is a mineral composed primarily of sodium chloride and is one of the universal tastes in fast food. It is an important food preservative. Salt regulates the fluids in our body and every living creature needs sodium and chloride, plants and animals alike, but only in small amounts.

It's a crystalline solid, white or sometimes pale pink or light grey and is processed from sea water or rock deposits. The greyish colour in edible rock salt comes from the mineral content of the rock and this is different to mineral salt that comes from plant sources (celery is the most common, it makes a superb salt alternative and the minerals in celery help balance the body).

Salt is such a valuable commodity it has been used as a currency in trade. Roman soldiers were paid in salt, in Greece slaves were traded for salt, in Ethiopia salt bars were stand currently until quite recently, hence the sayings, 'not worth one's salt' or 'the salt of the earth'.

We only need a very small amount of salt in our diets, preferably sea salt, and too much salt in your diet may cause dark circles under your eyes.

Salt used for human consumption comes in three forms: unrefined salt (sea salt), refined salt (table salt) and iodised salt. Sea salt is the most beneficial because it has the ability to restore balance to our body fluids, unlike table salt which is refined by adding aluminosilicate or sodium, or yellow prussiate of soda plus bleaches to make sure the salt is free flowing. The problem here is that this free-flowing salt is unable to combine with human body fluids.

Salt also makes us thirsty, which is why it's used as an ingredient in soft drinks—the answer to why soft drinks don't necessarily quench your thirst.

Salt has many uses and some surprising applications. It can be died and used to create artwork. It's a great way to keep an artificial floral arrangement in place—just fill your vase with salt, add a little bit of cold water and put your floral arrangement together. The salt will set hard as it dries keeping the flower in place.

The old wives' tale of making water boil faster by putting a pinch of salt into the pot doesn't hold water (pardon the pun), however a pinch of salt in water does make water boil at a higher temperature, which is why salted water works so well with poaching eggs—it raises the temperature and sets the whites faster.

Salt is not only a magic enhancer for boiling, it also works with freezing. If you're planning on going fishing and want to keep your cooler extra cold, or if you're camping and don't want to end with a slurry of ice but want chilled food, make your own long lasting ice blocks by mixing 1 cup of salt with approximately 2 litres of water, pour into large containers and keep in the home freezer until needed.

Adding salt to the ice block causes a temperature drop that slows the melting rate and increases the freezing rate; this is how old-fashioned ice cream makers lowered the temperature of the ice cream below water's freezing point. A mixture of rock salt, ice and water packed in the bucket around the ice cream mix can bring the temperature down as low as -21°C.

Salt is also a wonderful ingredient for cleaning products, it's cheap, easy to store and has a million and one uses.

The versatility of tea tree oil

Tea tree oil is obtained by steam distilling the leaves of the tea tree (*Melaleuca alternifolia*)—not to be confused with the unrelated common tea plant (*Camellia sinensis*) that is used to make black and green tea. The tea tree is native to Queensland and New South Wales in Australia. It was named by eighteenth century sailors who made tea that smelled like nutmeg from the leaves of the tree growing on the marshes and swamps of the southeast Australian coast.

Thought of as a natural cure-all, the chemicals in tea tree oil may kill bacteria and fungus and reduce allergic skin reactions. Tea tree oil contains *terpenoids*, which are chemically modified *terpenes*—organic compounds found to have antiseptic and antifungal activity. The compound *terpinen-4-ol* is the most abundant terpene in tea tree leaves and is thought to be responsible for most of the essential oil's antimicrobial activity. Tea tree oil is a common ingredient in deodorants, shampoos, soaps and lotions.

Tea tree oil is applied to the skin (used topically) for infections such as acne, fungal infections of the nail (*onychomycosis*), lice, scabies, athlete's foot (*tinea pedis*), and ringworm. It is also used topically as a local antiseptic for cuts and abrasions, burns, insect bites and stings, boils, toothache, infections of the mouth and nose, and sore throat, among other ailments. Some people add it to bath water to treat cough, bronchial congestion and pulmonary inflammation, although eucalyptus oil might be a more powerful respiratory remedy.

Tea tree oil is safe for most people when applied to the skin, but it can cause skin irritation and swelling in some cases, especially in large doses. For people treating acne, it can sometimes cause skin dryness, itching, stinging, burning and redness. Occasionally, people may have allergic reactions to tea tree oil, ranging from mild contact dermatitis to severe blisters and rashes. Undiluted tea tree oil may cause skin irritation, redness, blistering and itching.

Warning: Please be advised Tea tree oil is highly toxic to both humans and pets if ingested. NEVER USE ON ANY ANIMAL (as they can lick and digest it) OR IN OIL BURNERS AROUND ANIMALS.

Although its low toxicity and wide range of applications make it an ideal natural remedy, tea tree oil can have side effects. Studies show that contact with tea tree oil may alter hormone levels, causing unexplained breast enlargement in boys who have not yet reached puberty. People with hormone-sensitive cancers or pregnant or nursing women should avoid tea tree oil. It is unsafe when taken by mouth (orally). As a general rule, never take tea tree oil or any undiluted essential oils by mouth due to the possibility of serious side effects. Taking tree tea oil orally has caused confusion, inability to walk, unsteadiness, rash, and coma.

UNDILUTED TEA TREE OIL

+ A few drops of tea tree oil in your dishwasher dispenser will help remove the residue that builds up on your dishes.
+ Adding a few drops to your humidifier will not only emit a clean, refreshing scent into the air but it will also disinfect a sickroom (NEVER USE AROUND ANIMALS AS IT IS HIGHLY TOXIC TO PETS).
+ Add a few drops to your laundry as a freshener and disinfectant.
+ Tea tree oil is an excellent insect repellent. Wipe down your kitchen work surfaces and cabinets with a simple solution of soapy water and a few drops of tea tree oil to keep the bugs at bay. Do the same for any hard floors, paying attention the corners and trims. Your room will smell clean and the pests will stay away.

BASIC TEA TREE OIL SOLUTION

Use this solution as a room deodoriser, mildew repellent (though it will not remove previous discoloration from grout), a disinfectant spray or as a mould remover (do not wipe away).

Mix 15 drops of tea tree oil per 500ml of water, pour into a spray bottle and shake well.

COSMETIC USES

Simple healing ointment: Mix 5ml of a non-allergenic cream base, such as calendula cream, with 2 or 3 drops of tea tree oil and rub on affected areas such as cuts, blisters or rough patches of skin.

Scalp rub/dandruff treatment: To condition your hair and scalp as well as to combat dandruff and itchy scalp, rub 10 drops of tea tree oil with your fingertips into the scalp between shampoos.

Shaving rash: Characterised by a mass of small red pimples on the face and neck, it is exacerbated by shaving, of course. To counteract the irritation caused by your razor, rinse the affected areas with warm water containing a few drops of tea tree oil. For a more direct approach, add 10 to 12 drops of tea tree oil to a 50ml bottle of lavender water* and shake well. Dab the affected areas with the solution using cotton balls.

*Please refer to the Aromatherapy section of this book (p.118) for a simple lavender water recipe.

Eucalyptus: A miracle evergreen

Eucalyptus is a genus of flowering trees and shrubs in the myrtle family. Nearly all eucalyptus trees are evergreen (having leaves all seasons), but some tropical species lose their leaves after the dry season ends. Most species of eucalyptus are native to Australia, though they are cultivated throughout the world in temperate climates where it does not frost. They are fast-growing producers of wood, and their copious consumption of water makes them a natural insecticide because they drain swamps that attract mosquitoes, which spread malaria. The Australian Blue Mountains take their name from the haze created by the mist emitted by the trees' vaporising leaves, which contain ample amounts of volatile (rapidly evaporating) oil.

Eucalyptus trees are a source of pulpwood, which is converted into the pulp used to make paper. Their trunks, when hollowed out by termites, are used to make the didgeridoo, a traditional Aboriginal wind instrument, and the nectar of certain species is used to produce high quality honey. All parts of the eucalyptus can be used to produce dyes in colours ranging from yellow, orange and red to green, tan and rust.

Eucalyptus oil is distilled from the tree's leaves and has many medicinal and household uses such as relieving congestion and disinfecting clothing and surfaces. In addition to the applications for eucalyptus oil found throughout the book, its industrial applications include serving as a fragrance component in soaps, detergents and perfumes, as well as an ingredient in ethanol and petrol fuels.

Its health and beauty properties are discussed in the Aromatherapy section of this book (p.118), but here is an easy recipe for a natural, eucalyptus-based insect repellent. Spray it on yourself and around the outdoor area where you plan to camp or picnic. The scent of eucalyptus should keep the mosquitoes and ticks away, and it is safe to use around children and pets. Just remember to keep it away from your eyes.

NOTE: Eucalyptus oil is also toxic to dogs and cats. Never use any oils on animals unless checked by vet first.

EUCALYPTUS INSECT REPELLENT SPRAY
500ml water
2 capfuls (or 10ml) liquid soap (see page 26)
10-25 drops eucalyptus oil
Dark spray bottle

Mix the ingredients and pour them into the spray bottle, making sure to shake the contents before each use. Reapply every hour and after swimming or exercise.

Grapefruit: lemon's powerful cousin

The existence of the grapefruit tree was first documented in Barbados, where it was known as the 'forbidden fruit'. Like its citrus cousin the lemon it is a wonder fruit as all parts of the grapefruit have uses. The pulp is consumed whole and also squeezed for its tangy juice. It is a good source of vitamin C, and the pink and red varieties contain the antioxidant lycopene, which helps to remove free radicals—thought to cause many cancers—from your body. Lycopene is also believed to play a role in the prevention of heart disease by preventing LDL cholesterol from being oxidised. And most anyone who's attempted to eliminate that 'spare tire' knows that grapefruit's low glycemic index helps the body's metabolism burn fat.

Grapefruit seed extract (GSE), also known as citrus seed extract, is believed to have strong antimicrobial properties against fungi and bacteria. It is a liquid derived from the seeds, pulp, and white membranes of the grapefruit. Homemade GSE can be produced by grinding the seed and juiceless pulp of the grapefruit and mixing them with glycerine, but the process can be fairly difficult. Commercially manufactured GSE will suit your needs just fine.

GSE NATURAL CLEANER AND SANITISER

Use this mixture as a natural means of preventing the spread of E. coli, Salmonella, Staphylococcus, Streptococcus and other bacteria and germs. It also cleans and brightens hard surfaces.

Mix 15 drops of GSE per 500ml of water. (Double the amount of GSE per 500ml of water for heavy-duty jobs.) Pour into a spray bottle and use the solution to disinfect things such as plastic children's toys, playpens, doorknobs and garbage bins. Spray the solution onto your sinks, tubs and tiles, allowing it to sit for at least 15 seconds. Wiping the solution away should reveal whiter and brighter surfaces.

GRAPEFRUIT JUICE HOUSEHOLD CLEANSER

If you read the ingredient list on expensive commercial cleaners, you'll notice that many manufacturers use grapefruit in their products. Using fresh juice in a homemade alternative will give you pure cleaning power. You will still get the anti-viral and anti-microbial properties of the commercial cleansers, while making a product that is safe for children and pets and avoiding the unwanted respiratory reactions commercial cleaners can induce. Use this mixture to clean work surfaces, tubs, sinks and hard floors.

It is also ideal for items children comes into contact with like toys, cribs and any other sensitive areas.

Combine one part freshly squeezed grapefruit juice with one part vinegar and three parts hot water. Wipe down or mop surfaces and let air dry.

A STITCH IN TIME SAVES NINE: SIMPLE CLEANING HACKS

A stitch in time saves nine, as the famous saying goes, and never has it been more spot on than when it comes to cleaning. Lots of commercial cleaners lure you in to purchase them by claiming to 'cut through grease' but if you wipe down your surfaces each time you use them there will never be a build-up and therefore you will never need strong chemicals or industrial strength cleaners to 'cut' through anything.

This doesn't mean becoming a cleaning fanatic, more so getting in the habit and mind space to spare a few extra minutes at the end of other jobs or when you are feeling a bit motived but don't want to start a big job.

Most of us don't fantasise about spending hours cleaning but little jobs done regularly mean that you won't have to spend all Saturday morning doing the house cleaning and you can spend that time doing something fun instead.

Some tips that I have learnt that get the motivation juices flowing to do the little 'stitch in time' jobs are **time how long things take and focus on that**.

For example: wiping down the oven and kitchen benches each night may only take 7 minutes (not 10 minutes and only slightly more than 5 minutes) but when I don't feel like doing it, I tell myself this is only a 7-minute job! I do not think about the cleaning part, just that I have a spare 7 minutes and if done now that will save me half an hour at the end of the week.

This technique also works a treat on any jobs that tend to get put off because they are not fun. I tell myself that I will do a 15-minute job and that is it! So, I find a little job that I have put off and spend a spare 15 minutes on it. It makes it easier to start and to stop.

This technique has become so successful that I have even convinced family and friends to help if they are around by telling them it's only a 15-minute job, any chance of hand? And we can then be done in 10! Often you end up wanting to spend a little more time to finish it or start a new job if you get done early. This has become a catch phrase around our house and many of my friends have adopted it and love it!

It's great for kids and partners too! Asking someone to help 'clean the bathroom' has a whole different ring to it than 'can you help me with this 10-minute job then we are off to do fun things'.

Here is a list of perfect 5-minute jobs that require no arduous prepping or long packing up at the end and can help you with your 'stitch in time saves nine' cleaning tasks and buying and using extra and unnecessary chemicals in your home! Just remember to focus on the time they take rather than the task itself!

5-minute jobs in the kitchen

Choose any of the below, this is not a cleaning list just a 5-minute job that is exactly that! Start it and finish it in 5 minutes then walk away. It will save you money each week with cleaning products and save you time when you are doing a bigger clean each week.

+ Fill your sink with hot soapy water (dish liquid is perfect and if it's good enough for your dishes that you eat off its good enough for so many other areas that you touch, it's made to cut through grease and be gentle on your hands and the environment) and grab a cleaning cloth. I keep spare and old ones under my sink for these exact jobs, they can be washed in your washing machine and you can get so many uses out of them before they deteriorate. Give your work bench and area around and in your sink a good clean and wipe down! Remember to rinse your cloth and change your water often. You want steaming hot, soapy and clean water.

+ Pull your stove top knobs off and drop them in the sink, while you wipe down the stovetop, let the knobs soak and then wipe them down and put them back on. Your stovetop will always look sparkly clean and it is such a quick job but not one you may feel like doing after a few hours of cleaning.

+ Lift the hobs (the elements on the top of your stove if you have them) and take out the metal trays under them. Wrap them in aluminium foil and put them back. This will collect all the overflow and debris that falls out of your saucepans and fry pans. Simply replace the foil every week and you won't ever have to scrub the metal trays again.

+ Wipe down your splashback with lots of hot soapy water and give it a good dry with paper towel. It's amazing how much can splash everywhere! (Hence the name, splashback!)

+ Wipe your fridge door handles and your cupboard door handles down. These can harbour lots of germs from dirty hands and also bacteria from cooking. It is such a quick job to do when the sink is full of hot soapy water and gives your kitchen a sparkling clean appearance.

+ Wipe down your kettles and toaster (make sure you disconnect them at the power first).

+ Pop half a lemon in the microwave in a microwave safe bowl and turn it on for one minute. The steam and lemon will fill the microwave and make any stuck-on food very easy to wipe down with hot soapy water (throw the lemon away afterwards and be very careful of the hot bowl before you handle it).

+ Fill your sink with warm water and add ¼ cup bleach then soak your tea cups for 10 minutes. This works on anything that has been stained with tea or coffee. Rinse well with hot soapy water afterwards.

+ Disconnect your toaster and empty all the crumbs, these are a huge burning hazard and it is such a quick and easy job to do in less than 5 minutes!

+ Wipe down any light switches with a damp hot cloth, then dry with some paper towel. Just like kitchen cupboards and fridge doors, these can harbour lots of germs! (make sure your cloth is not too wet, as it can leak into the power source).

+ Grab half a lemon and give your chopping boards a good rub down with it, squeezing as much juice as you can into it as you go. Leave for a few minutes then give it a good scrub in fresh hot soapy water and leave to dry either in the Sun or in an extremely low oven (oven for wood boards only!).

+ Wipe down your salt and pepper grinders and anything else that you use often.

5-minute jobs in the bathroom

Just like in the kitchen, fill your bathroom sink with hot soapy water. Dish liquid works just as well in the bathroom. I also have a separate cleaning cloth under the sink that is easy to grab and use only for the bathroom.

+ Lift everything off your bathroom vanity counter and give each item a wash in the hot soapy water (just like doing the dishes but with your soap dish, toothbrush container, soap dispenser and even your hairbrush handles, combs etc.). Change the water regularly and refill with fresh hot water once done.

+ While all your bathroom items are drying, give the vanity a good wipe down and with a hot soapy cloth get into the crevices of your taps. I find a to and fro works perfectly (imagine flossing your teeth but with the cloth around your taps). Dry well with paper town and instead of wasting the damp paper towel, use it to wipe down any mirrors.

+ Give the door handles and light switch a good wipe down, same as in the kitchen. These items often get forgotten and can be a real centre for toilet germs etc.

+ Have a look under your vanity and throw away any old shampoo bottles etc.

+ Refill your bin liners with several at a time so when you are in a hurry you can pull your rubbish out and have the next one lined and ready (ideally with paper bags or eco-friendly composting options).

+ Pour some bi-carb down your shower drain (½ cup will work if it's not blocked) then turn on the hot water until all the bi-carb is gone.

5-minute jobs for other areas of the house

Once again hot soapy water with washing up detergent is suitable for simple jobs around the house and has no aggravating effects on the quality of air in your house. Grab a bucket and a cloth, I like to keep mine in the laundry ready to go so these jobs really only take 5 minutes!

Sugar soap also works wonderfully but does have a bleach effect, is harsher on your hands (wear gloves and avoid contact with your eyes, dilute according to packet instructions) and is best only used on walls and floors.

+ Wipe all the door handles and light switches around the house, as mentioned previously, the number of dirty hands that touch these each day would surprise you! Dry with paper towel afterwards.

+ Wipe down all surfaces that you see! Literally walk around the house with your bucket of hot soapy water and your cloth and wipe as many surfaces as you can in 5 minutes. Dusting just lifts the dust and it settles again somewhere else. Wiping down surfaces means the surface is as clean as your dishes that you eat off would be.

Remember to get the water as hot as you are comfortable to handle and to rinse your cloth after each item you have wiped.

+ Give your bedside tables (if you have them) a good clean and wipe down and shake off any dust that may be gathering on books etc. It will make the air while you are sleeping much cleaner and you will get a better night's sleep.

+ If it is a hot sunny day, take all your pillows outside and give them a good bake in the Sun! This is also great for doonas, blankets, winter jackets or anything that needs a good air out and refresh.

+ Water all your indoor plants. A quick way to do lots in one go and clean all their leaves is to pop them all in the shower and turn the water on (cold water only and gentle pressure) and give them a wash and soak at the same time. Then leave them to drain for a while and put them back all refreshed and happy. It also cleans their leaves!

+ Take your rubbish bins outside and soak them for 5 minutes with hot water and bleach—a 50/50 ratio works well (only use on plastic bins that you don't mind getting bleached). If you don't have bleach you can either drop the some lemon slices in the water (the ones you used above to clean the microwave are ideal) or just plain dish washing liquid will work. You do not need much water, just fill them to ⅓ full of hot water and leave for 5 minutes then give them a good swish around to clean the sides and pour the water out. One of the best reasons to NOT use harsh chemicals is that you can freely drain your cleaning water anywhere and even on your plants (not bleach water) and it's non-toxic and harmless for the environment.

+ Pour boiling water from a kettle onto any weeds growing through your pavers.

+ Take any couch/sofa cushions outside and air them out by laying them on the clothesline or on a seat in the Sun. Make sure to turn them and do not leave them in the Sun for too long if they have dark fabric as the Sun will bleach them.

+ Air your house out! Open all your doors and windows and let fresh air flush any stale air out (hot sunny days are perfect for this).

+ Shake outdoor mats and rugs. The old-fashioned way of beating them with a broom still works the best but cover your face as lots of dust can come out.

+ Give your vacuum cleaner filters a good clean and leave to dry. Next time you're vacuuming your vacuum will have full suction and use less power.

+ Do a quick walk around your house and turn off any unused power points and unplug any unused devices. Wipe down the power points with a damp cloth then dry with paper towel. This will save you more power than you could imagine and extend the life of your devices.

+ Give any bookcases a quick tidy up and maybe put out any new pictures or trinkets that you would like to display.

+ Air out pet beds and give any pet water bowls a good clean in hot water and refill.

+ Hose out your trash/rubbish/wheely bins and lean them on their side to drain well.

+ Wipe down your TV and picture frames so they are crystal clear.

+ Pour some bi-carb, vinegar and boiling water down your drains to give them a good clean.

+ Pull your blankets and doonas back from your bed and sprinkle some bi-carb over your mattress. Leave for a few minutes then vacuum it up to refresh and remove dead skin cells and mites.

+ Rinse out any bird feeders or water bowls (remember dirty bird feeders can cause diseases in birds that can kill them, so if you don't have time to change and clean the feeders regularly, best to leave them empty after you have cleaned them).

As you can see there is so many 5 minute jobs that can be done that help you not only save money but also get rid of bacteria, freshen the air and save you time at the end of a big house clean, plus they save you needing to buy extra products when shopping (because the jobs are small and done regularly they never need the commercial grade cleaners), they save plastic AND because they only take 5 minutes they are easy to do anytime!

You can even do a few while the kettle is boiling for a cuppa or while you're waiting for friends to come over. Each one of the jobs above will make your home fresher and healthier and they use only basic dishwashing liquid or other household items and a little elbow grease. Give it a go and I bet you will get addicted to the 5-minute job attitude. Before you know it, you will be doing 5 or even 10 and 15-minute jobs!

It's surprisingly satisfying cleaning for only 5 minutes, you can even write a list of your own and stick it to your fridge and offer the kids pocket money. So many ideas, so little time!

GENERAL CLEANING

Can 'hard water' affect appliances?

Yes. The minerals from hard water bond to the elements in appliances that use water, hampering their function. This hardening is called *calcification*. Over time, you may notice white deposits coming through the holes in the soleplate (or face plate) of your iron, or the coffee you brew each morning might begin to take on an unpleasant taste or take noticeably longer to brew. Once again—blame hard water!

To keep your coffee tasting delicious, periodically fill the reservoir of your brewer halfway with vinegar and run the coffee maker as normal (without coffee, of course). The vinegar will act as a decalcifying agent that removes the build-up. Then, fill the reservoir full of water and run it again to remove any trace of vinegar. Depending on how often you brew coffee and how hard your tap water is, you may need to perform this *decalcification* as often as once a month.

To prevent further white deposits from forming on your iron, first, clean the soleplate with a paste of vinegar and baking soda to remove any dirt, and wipe it clean. Then, repeat the same steps as recommended for the coffee maker, only with a combination of vinegar and water, allowing the liquid to steam for several minutes. Once you unplug the iron, make sure to pour out any unused liquid.

To keep the iron deposit-free, run distilled water rather than tap water through its steaming element during subsequent use, making sure after each use to pour out the unused water once you've unplugged the iron. Distilled water is simply water that has been purified by boiling the water into vapour so that its impurities are left behind and then condensing the vapour into a clean container, a process called – you guessed it – *distillation*. If you use water without impurities in your steam iron, white spots on the soleplate should become a thing of the past in no time.

No Streak Window Cleaner

Forget the fancy, highly perfumed and toxic commercial glass cleaners; nothing beats the old-fashioned methods. You can have windows glistening like diamonds with a few basic household ingredients.

¼ cup white vinegar
1 tbsp cornflour
1 litre warm water

Put all the ingredients into a spray bottle, give it a good shake to make sure everything is combined, spray onto the area to be cleaned and wipe off with crumpled newspaper or paper towel.

Note: Some newspapers don't work as a wipe for windows because the printers have changed the ink.

Or

For a simpler method mix 1 tbsp of cornstarch in 1 litre of warm water in a spray bottle. Spray and wipe. You'll need to rub a bit more if the vinegar is not added but the results will be just as good.

General window cleaners

Mix 2 tbsp of borax in 3 cups of water, spray and rub with dry newspaper.

Or

Clean windows with methylated spirits and dry newspaper.

You can use paper towel to dry the glass but newspaper leaves a film that keeps the window clean and streak free—squeaky clean, you'll actually hear the squeak as the paper runs across the glass.

Why does newspaper clean so well?

Unlike higher quality paper, newsprint contains no solid components like calcium carbonate or silica, which can scratch glass. Newsprint also leaves minimal lint behind because its individual fibres are more rigid and will not separate as easily as they would from a paper towel, which is more flexible. Additionally, highly polished glass is not absorbent; it actually repels water, whereas newsprint is highly absorbent. When you spray glass cleaner onto a mirror or window, the dirt on the glass clings to the liquid glass cleaner, which is absorbed by the newsprint, and voila! Spotless, scratch-free windows and mirrors!

But take note, while the ink from newsprint will not rub off on glass, it will most likely stain your hands and fingers, so wear rubber gloves if this is a concern.

Foaming Carpet Cleaner

¼ cup liquid soap (see page 26)
3 tbsp water

Whip the ingredients in a bowl with a beater until it foams then rub the foam into the carpet and rinse with water. Always test a corner before attacking the main part of the carpet.

To remove carpet stains

Red wine can be removed by rubbing either bicarb soda or salt on the stain, both are excellent absorbers.

Soak up as much of the wine as possible by pressing with a paper towel or cloth (anything absorbent—the shirt of the person who spilled the wine would be perfect!). Cover with either bicarb soda or salt, leave for a while until the remaining wine has been absorbed, leave until dry then vacuum.

If the spill is substantial you may need two applications of the bicarb or salt before vacuuming. Wait until the bicarb or salt has absorbed as much of the wine as it can, scrape the mess off using a knife or spoon, then finish the process.

Herbal carpet freshener

Bicarb soda is a superb stain remover and deodoriser, mix it with some essential oils and you have a perfect powder to freshen your carpet. Store in a large jar and if you leave the jar sitting in the corner you have a room freshener as well. Mix and match to suit your needs but here are a few suggestions to start with.

1 cup bicarb soda
½ cup lavender flowers

1. Crush the lavender flowers to release their scent before placing in the bicarb soda and putting into a large jar.
2. Shake vigorously to distribute the lavender scent.
3. Sprinkle the powder over the carpet, leave for 15 minutes and vacuum.

Or

1. Mix 4 cups of bicarb soda with 35 drops of eucalyptus oil and 30 drops of lavender oil (any combination is fine—this is just a guide).

2. Mix everything together in a bowl, breaking up any chunks that form and store in a large jar.

3. Sprinkle on the carpet, leave for 15 minutes before vacuuming.

To remove indentations in wool carpets

Put a cloth (a tea towel is perfect) over the indentation to protect the carpet then press with a warm iron. The heat from the iron will get the fibres standing up like a line of little soldiers.

Warning: don't use this trick on carpet with synthetics in it, it will melt the fibres and you'll have a patch that looks like dead soldiers on the battle field.

To remove animal hair from carpet and furnishings

We all love to drag our furry friends up onto our laps for cuddle time but the hair left behind (especially in moulting season) is no joy at all. A quick and easy way to get cat and dog hair out of fabrics or carpets is to rub the area with dampened rubber gloves. A gentle pat with the rubber glove treatment will keep your pets free from loose hair.

Floor Cleaner

Add white vinegar into the rinse water after you've washed your floors, the vinegar will help stop dirt or grease sticking to the floor (great for kitchen floors) and if you're into polishing your floors try using a bit of skim milk on the floor (after the floor has dried), it will polish to a beautiful shine.

To hide scratches on ceramic and marble floors

Spray with WD40 and the marks will disappear.

Furniture polish for wood furniture

Mix olive oil and lemon juice at a ratio of 2:1. Gently rub the mixture over the wood, let stand for several hours then polish with a soft cloth.

Or

Mix the juice of 1 lemon with 1 tsp of olive oil and 1 tsp of water. Pour onto a soft cloth, apply a thin coat to your wood surfaces, leave for 5 minutes and use a clean soft cloth to buff it off. This is best made fresh for each use.

To hide scratches on your wood furniture

Take the meat of a walnut (the part we eat) and cut it in half. Rub the soft inside part of the nut over the scratches, this works like walnut oil but you need to use whole fresh nuts you have cracked to get the best results. Most walnuts on the supermarket shelves are quite old and they don't have the same level of fresh oil, but in a pinch they would do if you can't get your hands on the whole nut.

To remove watermarks on wood furniture

Rub the affected area with toothpaste. Toothpaste is also good for cleaning silver.

To remove crayon marks from walls

If darling little Johnny has discovered the joy of scribbling on your walls with crayon just spray the crayon with WD40 and wipe with a clean rag. Works wonders.

Marble

Marble is porous and can stain very easily. To protect a marble surface from staining polish it with a clear car polish, it leaves a thin film for protection.

Air fresheners

The commercial air fresheners are designed to cover-up smells, one layer on another.

The best way to keep a house smelling clean and fresh is to open the windows regularly to give the house a good airing but if you like a slight fragrance throughout the house trying simmering some cinnamon sticks, orange peel and a few cloves in water, strain, and spray where needed. A word of warning: check that the spray won't stain or damage areas like carpets, curtains etc.

Or

Collect rose petals that have a strong fragrance. Layer the petals with salt in an attractive jar with a tight-fitting lid. Take the lid off when you want to freshen up the room. Seal in between uses.

Or

Use a cotton swab to apply a drop of your favourite essential oil on a light bulb, when you turn your lights on the heat from the bulb will fill the room with a lovely fragrance.

Or

Mix water and vinegar in a 1:1 ratio, add 10 drops of lavender oil, store in a squirt bottle and spray as needed.

Simple Metal Cleaners

NON-TOXIC SILVER CLEANER

All metals (with the exception of gold) rust or corrode with exposure to oxygen through a process that involves electrons moving between the metal and oxygen atoms. It's a pretty spontaneous reaction and silver tarnish is only different because of the combination of sulphur rather than oxygen. It's a bit more of a complex reaction but the principle that tarnishes silver is the same that rusts iron.

The salt water and aluminium trick is the result of a simple chemical reaction called 'ion exchange' whereby the tarnish on the silver is transferred to the foil with the salt water acting as the conductor.

If you are cleaning silver that is heavily tarnished you'll be able to see the brown tarnish that has jumped across to the foil. Neat trick hey?

1. Rustle up some tarnished silver.
2. Take some aluminium foil and fold it a few times to make a square mat (shiny side facing outwards).
3. Put the foil into a bowl of warm salted water.
4. Immerse your silver and leave for a while.
5. Remove, dry with a soft cloth.

And you guessed it—perfectly cleaned silver with no rubbing, no polishing, and no nasty chemicals. All for the princely sum of 1 cent worth of aluminium foil and a little bit of salt.

Or

Use toothpaste, an old soft bristled toothbrush and water. Pretend you are brushing your teeth. The toothpaste will do a brilliant job of cleaning the silver—it's gentle on the silverware and if you make sure you use a soft bristled brush there is no risk of damage or scratching.

Or

Rub with a paste of bicarb soda and water, rinse then dry with a soft cloth.

Or

Soak in hot salty water that has had a strip of aluminium foil placed in the bottom. Leave for about 10–20 minutes. Lift the silverware out and dry with a soft cloth.

BRASS

Mix equal parts salt and flour with a small amount of vinegar, rub the mixture on the brass then buff clean with a dry soft cloth.

CHROME

Rub with undiluted white vinegar then polish with a soft dry cloth.

COPPER

Rub with lemon juice and salt—or hot vinegar and salt. Either one will work. Rub with a dry soft cloth.

STAINLESS STEEL

Rub with a paste of baking soda and water, rinse, buff with a dry soft cloth.

Removing rust stains

Because rust is formed through corrosion it is extremely hard to get rid of but that doesn't mean it's not worth trying. Here is one way you can attack the problem—once the rust is removed make sure you seal the area otherwise the cycle will start again as the oxygen begins a new corrosion activity.

Scrub with a stiff or metal brush making sure you remove all traces of rust then cover the area with a sealant.

Rust can only survive where there is oxygen (which is why items at the bottom of the ocean can stay rust free for generations); starve the area of oxygen and you won't have any further problems.

To make candles last longer

Some candles these days seem to go up in smoke in a matter of minutes. To make them last longer seal them in a plastic bag, or wrap them in glad wrap, and leave them in the freezer overnight.

Make candles drip free

Don't waste money on expensive dripless candles. Buy the el-cheapo candles and soak them in a solution of equal parts water and salt for a few hours, remove, let dry before you light them and they'll burn as usual but won't drip candle wax.

To remove residue from stickers or duct tape

Wipe with tea-tree oil, eucalyptus or WD40. WD40 is the most effective to remove duct tape residue.

Removing glue from hands

For the home handyman who is a bit careless with super glue try rubbing some peanut butter into the area then wipe it off with a cloth. Simple but works wonders.

KITCHEN

Simple homemade liquid detergent

1. Decant 500ml of liquid soap (see page 26)
2. Store in a squeeze top bottle and use as needed. A few big squirts will do a large wash and if you want loads of suds squirt the liquid directly under the tap and turn the tap on full. The stronger the water pressure, the more bubbles you'll get.

If you are in an area where the water is hard, add 2 tbsp of washing soda dissolved in 1/4 cup of water to the soap mixture, and if you have greasy washing up to do add 2 tbsp of bicarb to the liquid soap or the juice of half a lemon.

Now the thing about homemade washing up detergent is that it may not be 100% streak free. It won't be far off but there could be some residue on glassware, plates will be fine, but glassware may not gleam like diamonds without a bit of help. The chemical companies have it down pat; you literally don't need to dry your dishes because they do it for you in their formulation.

Any residue left on glassware can we wiped off quickly while the dishes are put away and here's where the old-fashioned tea towel comes into play. Manual wiping up is good bonding time for siblings, time for chatting about the day, sharing some juicy gossip from school, and with the prospect of a bit of tea towel flicking there's never an argument about who's on drying-up duty.

Basic all purpose kitchen and bench cleaner
½ tsp baking soda
½ tsp borax
2 tbsp vinegar
½ tsp liquid soap (see page 26)
2 cups water

1. Combine all ingredients in a spray bottle (feel free to use your previous all purpose cleaner bottle, just make sure it has been rinsed very well) and shake until and all the ingredients are combined.
2. Spray then wipe clean with a damp cloth.

Tips: You can a few drops of essential oil to give your cleaner a lovely scent. A tiny sprinkle of lemon rind is also a lovely natural scent to use.

If you find that you require stronger cleaning power, just increase the amount of borax by 1 tsp.

For a quick fix
Sprinkle bicarb soda onto the surface you want to clean. Spray with a solution of water and vinegar at a ratio of 1:3. Wipe dry.

For stubborn stains
For stubborn stains put a few drops of lemon juice on the stain and leave it to sit for a few minutes before sprinkling bicarb over and scrubbing gently. Rinse with water.

Kitchen cupboards
Use vinegar or lemon juice diluted in warm water to wipe spills and marks on cupboard shelves. The vinegar will kill any bacteria that may be lurking ready to multiply and it will also help prevent mould and mildew.

Usually ¼ cup of either vinegar or lemon juice together with 1 cup of warm water is a good ratio.

Drain cleaner
¼ cup bicarb soda
½ cup of white vinegar

Make sure the sink is dry (otherwise the bicarb clumps and is hard to get down the plug hole. If it clumps just break it up and push it through, it just takes a bit longer).

1. Pour the bicarb soda into the drain.
2. Pour the vinegar down the drain hole (a bit at a time).
3. Put the plug in and let everything sit for 15–30 minutes to work its magic then pour hot water down the drain to make sure everything is washed through.
4. If your drain is particularly sluggish you can repeat the process, the best way to know when to stop adding vinegar is when the fizzing stops.

To clean your microwave
2 tbsp of lemon juice or vinegar
4 cups of water

1. Mix water and lemon juice together in a large microwave safe bowl.
2. Microwave on high for 3–4 minutes.
3. Allow the steam to condense on the inside walls.
4. Remove the bowl (careful, it will be hot) and wipe the inside of the microwave with a clean cloth.
5. Repeat to get rid of stubborn spots.

To get rid of fingerprints on stainless steel fridges and ovens

To keep the fridge door free of fingerprints, wipe with a soft cloth that has been dabbed with a small amount of baby oil. Keep the cloth somewhere handy.

To remove magic marker from surfaces

Hopefully you won't encounter the accidental magic marker on bench surfaces very often as they can be hard to remove but try spraying the mark with hair spray then wipe it clean.

Powder for your dishwasher

Make up a powder for the dishwasher by mixing equal parts of bicarb with borax and use 2 tbsp per load.

Or

Mix 1 cup borax with 1 cup bicarb soda, ¼ cup of salt and ¼ cup of citric acid. You can also add a few drops of essential oils but this is optional.

Store in an airtight plastic container and use 1 tbsp per load.

Dishwasher odours and soap build-up

Splash 1 cup of vinegar around the inside of the empty machine then run a cycle without any dishes. If you do this once a month it will keep your machine smelling fresh and free from soap scum. It works just as well if you run it through a full load and saves wasting water.

To remove kitchen odours

No-one likes unpleasant smells wafting through the kitchen, here are a few tips for cheap and effective air fresheners.

REFRIGERATOR AND CUPBOARDS

Keep an open box of bicarb soda in your fridge, cupboards or any-where you would like to remove offending odours. Bicarb has the most amazing ability to absorb odours and will stay effective for ages. You can re-use the bicarb to make a cleaning paste or oven cleaner after it's done its job as an odour eater.

BENCH TOP COMPOST AND WHEELIE BINS

You can also sprinkle bicarb in your garbage cans and bench top compost bins to keep them smelling fresh.

FOOD CONTAINERS AND LUNCH BOXES

There are a few quick ways to get rid of the stale smell that builds up in re-used food containers and lunch boxes.

+ Soak a piece of sliced bread in vinegar and put it into the container, put the lid on and leave overnight. In the morning remove the bread and rinse the container under the tap.
+ Sprinkle bicarb soda around inside of the container and rinse in hot water. If the smell is particularly strong, rather than rinsing the container leave a mixture of water and bicarb in the container overnight and rinse in the morning.
+ Wipe the container over with a cloth drench in white vinegar then rinse.
+ If your container is microwave safe put some water into the container with half a lemon and microwave for 2 minutes on high, leave to cool before removing then wash in warm soapy water.

REMOVE ODOURS FROM JARS

If you keep glass jars for re-use but find some retain the smell of past ingredients simply pour some strong black coffee into the jar, put the lid on loosely, leave for a while, empty and rinse with water. Any odour will go out with the coffee. It's also a great way to use leftover coffee.

REMOVE ODOUR FROM YOUR GARBAGE DISPOSAL UNIT

Pour ½ cup of sea salt down your disposal followed by a few ice cubes then run the cold water and start the disposal. The ice will help dislodge all the chunky bits and the salt will remove odours.

TO GET RID OF THE LINGERING SMELL OF FISH

A thick fillet of fried fish makes a great meal but what isn't so great is the lingering fishy smell that permeates the kitchen and adjoining rooms; not quite up there with cooked cabbage but it gets pretty close.

Here's a handy tip to get rid of the fishy smell so you can enjoy your meal without having to breathe in the aftermath.

As soon as you take the fish out of the pan throw in a blob of peanut butter. Don't ask me how it works but it absorbs the lingering odour instantly.

GENERAL ODOUR-EATER

To mask general odours burn some coffee beans in a saucepan, but not enough to damage the saucepan. The strong coffee smell overpowers any other smell lurking around.

Ovens and stoves

Hate cleaning the oven? Most of us do.

Here are a few recipes for oven cleaners that work a treat, have a play around to find the one you prefer and when your oven is sparkling like new keep it that way by wiping it over with a cloth doused in vinegar after each use (preferably before it cools down completely). The vinegar stops fat sticking so your job becomes easier and easier—almost like a self-cleaning oven.

These recipes work as well if not better than the chemical oven cleaners on the market and best of all they're free from Butane, Monoethanolamine, Diethylene Glycol Monobutyl Ether, Sodium Hydroxide and Diethanolamine, which commercial products may contain. No-one need take the risk of breathing any of those into the lungs.

TO KEEP YOUR OVEN SPARKLING CLEAN AND GREASE FREE

Wipe the oven with a damp cloth soaked in diluted white vinegar. If you do this regularly the grease and fat from cooking won't stick to the oven walls and it will make it easier to keep clean.

It only takes a second to give the oven a wipe over and if you have just cleaned the oven with a strong-smelling cleaning agent the vinegar will get rid of the smell so it won't taint your next meal.

If there is some build-up on the oven walls or floor shake some bicarb soda onto a soft scourer and give it a quick wipe, then rise clean and finish off with a vinegar treatment.

OVEN DOOR

To clean a grease-splattered oven door, use a cloth saturated with white vinegar, full strength this time, wipe the problem area and leave the oven door open for 15-20 minutes before rinsing with a damp sponge.

TO CLEAN THE BOTTOM OF YOUR OVEN

This is always a problem area, especially if spilled food is left to re-bake (it's so much easier to wipe the oven clean after each use).

This is an easy remedy but before you start make sure the oven is cold and cover any elements with foil or something to protect them.

1. Using an atomiser full of water, spray the bottom of the oven.
2. Sprinkle bicarb soda over the oven floor.
3. Give it a few more squirts of water from the atomiser.
4. Leave overnight and wipe over with a damp cloth.
5. Rinse with hot water.

If the oven floor has a lot of caked on residue you may need to repeat this a few times.

Once the oven floor is clean give it a final rinse over with vinegar to stop grease sticking.

TO CLEAN A SPILL ON THE BOTTOM OF THE OVEN

We've all done it—had a casserole or pie bubble over spilling food all over the bottom of the oven. Best to attack it before it bakes and sets hard.

Cover the spill with a handful of salt. Salt doesn't smoke or smell under heat and it will bake into a crust that makes it easier to clean the mess up (but wait until it cools down, no point in burning your fingers).

TO CLEAN YOUR SINK

Nothing beats bicarb soda to give a mirror shine to your sink. Make a paste of bicarb soda and water and apply with a cloth then wipe over and rinse, or sprinkle bicarb soda directly onto a damp cloth, wipe over and then rinse off. Either method works well, it's just a matter of what suits you.

SCOURING POWDER

This is abrasive for those stubborn areas and is not suitable for laminated bench tops, glass top hot plates or any surface that might scratch.

Mix equal parts of bicarb soda, borax and salt together to use as a scouring powder to remove heavy grease and dirt.

TO REMOVE BURNT FOOD FROM COOKING PANS

One old fashioned cleaning method was to put burnt saucepans and dishes upside down on top of an ant hill and leave them for the industrious little fellows to slowly munch their way through the burnt food until the pans and dishes were clean. Worked well, but it took a while, here's an easier and faster method.

¼ cup bicarb soda
2 tbsp salt
Hot water (enough to make a thick paste)

1. Make a paste of the bicarb, salt and water.
Use a damp cloth and wipe the paste over the pan—or if you are

cleaning the oven over the walls of the oven (keep away from wires and heating elements).

2. Let the paste sit for at least 5–10 minutes (can leave for up to 20 minutes but make sure that the paste is not too dry to start with).

3. Rinse with warm water and a cloth.

For tough stains, scrub with fine steel wool and some more baking soda. It's always best not to use steel wool unless absolutely necessary, loosening grease and grime is always better for the surfaces than scrubbing, once they have been scrubbed they become harder to clean.

Or

Juice the stalks of some rhubarb to wipe over the burn or boil some chopped rhubarb in a very small amount of water, simmer gently, leave overnight then wipe clean.

AND SPEAKING OF BURNING

Salt always held a place of honour in Grandma's kitchen. The salt jar wasn't so much an indication of how much salt Granny used in cooking because salt has many uses as a scourer, mouth gargle, as well as an aid to cooking, and it was no accident that the salt pot was kept near the stove.

Salt is a brilliant fire extinguisher for grease fires, it acts like a heat blanket, dissipating the heat and starving the fire of oxygen. In an emergency a handful of dirt will do the same but by the time you've come back in from the yard the fire could well have taken hold.

So if you like homemade deep fried chips follow Granny's lead and keep a big accessible jar of salt near the stove just in case.

TO REMOVE GREASE FROM POTS AND PANS

Save yourself that awful job of getting grease out of pans and reduce water wastage at the same time. Simply sprinkle the pot, pan or BBQ plate with salt and leave it to do its job absorbing. Wipe with paper towel and you'll find all the grease will have been absorbed and you can wash your pan without contaminating the rest of the washing up with an unpleasant greasy film.

Kitchen windows, backsplashes and floors

Kitchen windows, backsplashes and kitchen floors all have one thing in common—they are the target for grease and fat splatters from cooking.

Vinegar stops grease and fat sticking and makes cleaning easier so use vinegar when you are cleaning glass or the backsplash and throw some in the final rinse when you're doing the floor and you'll find cleaning much easier the next time around.

KITCHEN DISINFECTANT
1 cup water
1 cup white vinegar
20-30 drops of tea tree or eucalyptus oil

Mix all ingredients together in a spray bottle and use when needed.

A FEW HELPFUL NOTES ON THE CARE OF WOODEN CUTTING BOARDS

Bacteria lives in the moisture that is on your boards, so make sure your boards are nice and dry when you're not using them. I lean mine up against the back of our drying rack so that only a small part of the board is touching the bench. This ensures that the whole board dries at the same time.

I only ever use my wood board for chopping vegetables, bread etc, but never meat. If I want to chop meat on it, I either cover my board with parchment paper so I can throw it away later or use some cheap plastic mats. I still use my wooden board underneath because I like the solid feel but the plastic mats can go in the dishwasher afterwards and my wooden board is safe from cross contamination.

Never leave your wooden boards submerged in hot water. Wood is porous and will soak up water, which is bad for cracking and also creates a breeding ground for bacteria.

TO CLEAN AND DISINFECT WOODEN CUTTING BOARDS

Use a spray bottle with full strength white vinegar. Vinegar is a fantastic disinfectant and will protect your wooden boards from the harmful bugs, E. coli, salmonella and staphylococcus, and it works on plastic cutting boards just as effectively.

TO REMOVE GARLIC AND ONION SMELLS FROM YOUR WOODEN BOARDS

Rub half a lemon over the board and wipe down with some paper towel.

Or

Rub your board with coarse salt or bicarb soda. Leave it for a few minutes then rinse.

Or

If you live somewhere sunny, once you have washed your board, put it out in sunlight for a few hours (make sure you turn it so both sides get a good hit of sunshine). Let the sunshine work its magic.

TO REMOVE GARLIC AND ONION SMELLS FROM YOUR HANDS

If your skin has picked up garlic or onion smells rub your hands on stainless steel before you wash them, the sink is ideal and you'll be surprised at how effective this trick is.

Alternatively, you can use lemon or bicarb. They will work just as well on your hands as they do on wooden cutting boards.

TO DISINFECT YOUR WOODEN SPOONS

Soak them in a ratio of 1 part bleach to 20 parts water for 15 minutes. Rinse and resoak in warm soapy water for 15 minutes to remove the bleach smell. Wash as normal and dry completely.

Your wooden spoons are similar to your cutting boards and will absorb some of the liquids they stir. It's a good idea to give them a good disinfecting every now and then, this will kill the bugs but also extend the lifespan of your utensils.

Avoid putting your wooden utensils in the dishwasher, it will shorten their lifespan and help absorb other contaminants that may be in your washing load.

TO EXTEND THE LIFE OF YOUR KITCHEN SPONGES

There is a lot of hype about the hygiene of using kitchen sponges. One ad would have us believe using a kitchen sponge is like wiping your benches with a piece of raw chicken. But there is nothing wrong with using sponges providing you are diligent with keeping them in good condition.

Here's a quick way to extend their life, save on paper towel use and also make sure that your sponges are hygienic.

Make up a solution of ⅓ cup of salt and ½ cup of vinegar per 1 litre of water. Soak your sponges overnight in this solution and they'll be restored to their former glory and be free from bacteria.

Germs love to live in warm, moist environments so when you're not using your sponges make sure you put them on your draining rack to dry thoroughly, also leave them out in sunlight as often as you can.

Here's another quick method for those with a microwave. Wet the sponge, squeeze the excess water out and put it in the microwave on high for 2 minutes. The heat will kill any bacteria but remember the sponges will be hot and will hold the heat for a while so wait until they have cooled before you attempt to take them out.

EASY METHOD TO CLEAN UP BROKEN EGGS

We've all tried to scoop up an egg that has dropped on the floor and struggled with getting the floor completely clean and disposing of the mess on the sponge. Here's a much easier way.

Cover the broken egg with salt and let the salt draw the egg together. Then just wipe it up with some paper towel.

EASY METHOD FOR PICKING UP BROKEN GLASS

If you have broken glass and are worried that you haven't picked up all of the splinters, use a thick piece of soft bread and wipe over the area where you think the glass may be. The bread will catch even the smallest splinters.

Please be sure you seal the glass laden bread before you discard it into the rubbish bin to avoid any hungry scavengers at the tip eating it.

TO REMOVE STAINS FROM COFFEE AND TEA CUPS OR A COFFEE POT

¼ cup salt
3 tbsp lemon juice or white vinegar
Some ice cubes

Mix all ingredients together in a pouring jug, pour some into each cup, swish the mixture around and rinse. The ice cubes combined with the salt and lemon/vinegar work together to remove any stains.

COOKERY HINTS AND TIPS

I have been in the food industry for over 23 years and some of the questions I get asked the most are sometimes the easiest tips to share. Below are a few cookery hints and tips that may help you save on mess and kitchen failures and save you some money along the way.

Eggs

Poached eggs: The best way to poach eggs is to use fresh eggs, there simply is no way to make an old egg have the effect you want as a poached egg unless it is fresh enough.

If you have an egg that is halfway between fresh or not, simply add a teaspoon of vinegar to the water and bring to a gentle simmer, make a circle in the water with a spoon, break your egg into a cup first and then gently release it into the pot of water.

The swirling motion of the water will hold your egg whites together. A fresh egg will always poach perfectly, just make sure the water is simmering, not boiling.

Another easy way is to put some water in a fry pan, so you have a bigger surface area, a great way if you are short on time. Gently crack your egg into the very shallow water pop a lid on your fry pan and turn the heat off, the heat of the already simmering water will cook them in a couple of minutes. You will have a flatter poached egg, but you will have nice clean egg whites.

Boiled eggs: What seems like the simplest thing in the world can actually be quite difficult. This is my tried and tested method that works every time.

Put the room temperature egg or eggs in a saucepan, cover with tap water, put on the stovetop at maximum heat, leave until it starts to boil. As soon as it comes to the boil turn the heat off, put a lid on the saucepan (leave on the hot element) and set your timer for 6 minutes.

This will give you an egg that has an incredibly soft yolk but set whites.

Boiled eggs for sandwiches: Once again fresh eggs work best, they always peel beautifully, the older the egg the harder it will be to work with, but any egg can be boiled easily by simply following the above method for 6 minutes.

Drain and rinse your eggs in cold water. You may have to do this several times as the egg will hold the heat for a while. Rinse until you get cool water and a cool egg. Drain all the water and gently shake your eggs around in your saucepan until all the shells have cracked around the outside, you should then be able to just peel all the shell off in one or two easy moves.

Easy scrambled eggs: The trick to not having watery scrambled eggs is to slightly undercook them. Heat your pan on heat, add a generous dollop of butter or olive oil, gently whisk your eggs with 2 tablespoons of milk in a separate cup or bowl and then pour into your fry pan. Don't stir! Over stirring will give you watery and pale looking scrambled eggs. Let your eggs almost completely set in the pan and then gently stir as little as possible to just get the mixture fluffy.

And that is all you need to do! take them off the heat while they still look slightly soft and runny as they will continue to cook with the heat in the pan while you make your toast and by the time you come back, you will have fresh delicious, scrambled eggs not watery at all.

Easiest sponge cake recipe: The trick to a great sponge cake is the time spent beating the eggs. If you do not have a handheld beater or mixer this recipe may not suit you.

This is my fail-safe sponge recipe that I use in my shop all the time, it's light and fluffy and never sinks!

4 eggs (large, fresh and room temperature)
Dash of vanilla essence
1 cup caster sugar
1 cup plain flour

1. Preheat the oven to 150°C (conventional oven), 130°C fan-forced, 300°F.
2. Put the eggs, vanilla and sugar in the bowl of a mixer and beat at maximum speed for at least 10 minutes, ideally 12 to 13 minutes.
3. Turn off the beaters and sift in the flour. Very gently fold the flour through until it is all combined.
4. Pour the mixture into a baking tray that has been sprayed and then coated in sugar (this will mean you will not need baking paper and it gives a beautiful meringue like coating around the outside and it will release beautifully).
5. Bake in the oven for 45 minutes. Gently remove from the oven and let it rest for five minutes before turning out of the tray. You should have a perfect sponge that will last three to four days if kept in an airtight container. This recipe also freezes perfectly!

Easy omelette: A problem most people have with omelettes is that they do not release from the pan. The trick is to gently fry any vegetables or other ingredients first in an oiled pan then set them aside on a plate. Add the scrambled egg mixture into the pan so it completely covers the bottom and leave to set for 2 or 3 minutes to cook and just slightly seal then add the vegetables and cheese over the top of the egg. Put a lid on the fry pan and turn the heat down to low and let it cook for 5 minutes. Your omelette will come out fluffy and light and release easily from the pan.

Egg shells: While we are on the subject of eggs, don't throw away your eggshells, they are fabulous for your garden and make wonderful nutrients for your soil. Simply put them in a container and leave in the Sun to dry out. Once they are dry, crumble them up and put them around things like lettuce or leafy greens or any plants that you have a problem with slugs. Slugs do not want to crawl over eggshells so they leave all your precious plants alone.

Checking egg freshness if you don't have a use-by date: Simply put your eggs in a very deep bowl of water—if they float they are off, get rid of them. If they are on their side, they are fine to eat. If they have turned up right but are not floating they're about a week old—it is an easy way to tell the freshness of your eggs.

Fruit and Vegetables

Fruit and vegetables are the highest waste product from grocery shopping. It seems crazy that we drive all the way to the shops to buy ourselves healthy fruit and vegetables just to shove them in the bottom of the crisper and then throw them away at the end of the week. The easiest way to avoid waste is with this handy tip.

When you buy your vegetables rinse them, dry them and then roughly chop them and put into a stainless-steel bowl in your fridge. You can cover with glad wrap or a damp tea towel. The stainless steel bowl will keep them fresh and crisp for longer and they will be chopped and ready to grab.

This hospitality trick works just as well for salads (just do not add any dressing until just before you want to eat it).

Having all your vegetables already chopped up ready to go means you will have no waste and you'll be saving on pre-packaged salads that use excess plastic. No more soggy carrots or sad looking salads!

RAW VEGETABLE SALAD

I use this recipe every week when I buy my vegetables and it is a life-saver on time and makes dinner so easy.

Whenever I buy my vegetables, I chop them all up roughly (see tip above). Cauliflower, broccoli, capsicums, carrots and anything except for strong smelling vegetables such as onions or starchy vegetables such as potatoes can be added to this salad.

Chop to whatever size you prefer—nice and fine or chunky if you like it that way. Store in stainless silver bowl in the fridge and use as a base for hundreds of recipes. Want to make a stir fry simply? Add two handfuls of this to your noodles and sauce. After a nice salad? Chop it up fine and add to lettuce and tuna. If you're having an omelette you can drop a handful of veggies in first. Making pasta sauce? Add a couple of handfuls and some tomato puree. For curries add your veggies and some curry pasty and rice.

I think you get the idea! the list goes on and on, this recipe works in so many dishes. All your vegetables are fresh and ready and in one bowl whenever you want them. You will have zero waste and the stainless steel bowl will keep it fresh for three times longer than the crisper. It's worth giving it a go, one big chop up and you have it ready for the rest of the week.

BANANAS

Never store bananas in the fridge. Ripe bananas will go black and green ones will not ripen properly after they are removed from the cold atmosphere.

Ripen green bananas by lightly wrapping them in a paper bag together with a couple of apples.

Freeze bananas in zip lock bags—flatten or squish them before putting in the freezer. It will make them much easier to use or break apart when frozen.

BEANS

When cooking beans do not cover them with a lid as they lose their colour. Most beans do well with just being soaked, rinsed with water and then gently simmered before use.

BOILING VEGETABLES

It is best to simply steam vegetables. They need very little water to cook as they contain a lot of water themselves. Simply add a small amount of water (¼ cup) to the bottom of a saucepan or fry pan then add all your vegetables and put a lid on. Put on rapid heat for 3–5 minutes—you'll see the colour starting to change as soon that happens. Turn off the heat and drain the water (the vegetables will continue to cook with the heat in the pan).

You would be amazed at how little time vegetables need to cook. This is why restaurants always have such vivid bright and crisp vegetables. Boiling removes all their nutrients.

MUSHROOMS

Many mushrooms are sold in plastic containers or in cardboard containers but wrapped in plastic. This is the worst way to store mushrooms as they will go slimy. The best thing to do with mushrooms is buy them loose in a paper bag—it is not only better for the environment, but your mushrooms will last a lot longer.

ONIONS

To stop onions making you cry when you cut them simply store them in the fridge or rinse under cold water once you have cut them. The cold and the water remove the chemical output that makes onions make people cry.

POTATOES

Never store potatoes and onions together. Don't store potatoes in plastic as they will rot. Unwashed potatoes will last a lot longer than washed ones and don't forget potatoes will go green in the light so store them in a dark place.

SPINACH

So many people throw the stalks of spinach out, is a total waste of a delicious part of the plant. Rinse and then thinly slice and add to stir fries—it has a similar texture to bok choy. Discard any particularly woody stems but the rest can all be eaten.

This rule also applies to broccoli and cauliflower—the stalks are delicious chopped up and added to stir fries, stews or casseroles. Don't discard these as they are a huge part of the nutritional value of the vegetable.

ZUCCHINI

Often when you see cheap zucchinis because they are in season and there is a glut of them. Zucchinis are fabulous to bulk up any dish and make a great freezer staple. You can get lots of zucchinis for very little money and they freeze beautifully along with silverbeet and other root vegetables.

Simply chop them up into small squares (no need to blanch beforehand) and put them in a freezer bag. When you're ready, bang the bag on the side of the table so they separate and pop them in your casseroles as a thickening agent. They will go slightly softer than if they were fresh but still add great texture to lots of things like rata-touille, curries, sauces etc.

SILVERBEET

As mentioned above, silverbeet freezes beautifully. Simply rinse in water, let dry and then shove the whole silver beet (stems and all, do not chop) into large freezer bags. When you are ready to use it simply crunch up the bag with your hand and you will get beautiful small pieces of silverbeet perfect for curries, stews and sauces.

MAKE YOUR OWN SALTS AND HERB RUBS

If you grow your own herbs you will have an abundance at certain times of the year. It's easy to dry these herbs out by hanging in a dry, cool place (or a dry oven that is still warm from dinner). When completely dried, add to salt and put in jars. Some great combinations are:

+ Rosemary and sea salt
+ thyme and sage salt
+ oregano and garlic salt just add dried garlic

The combinations are endless with whatever you have on hand and in the garden. You can add any of your favourite spices such as chilli or paprika and make delicious rubs to cook with. They also make great gifts.

TOMATOES

Tomatoes have so many uses but if you have a glut of tomatoes or they are very cheap at the store and you would like to make some delicious antipasto platter dips or pasta sauces, this is a very easy way.

Turn your oven on low and add the tomatoes to a roasting dish coated in olive oil. Sprinkle with some salt and pepper, a pinch of sugar and a little bit of balsamic vinegar. Bake for 30 minutes at a very low heat until they just start to soften, you will end up with a beautiful sauce or dish for a cheese platter that's always a hit.

LAUNDRY

Cheap and effective homemade laundry detergents

If we believed everything we see on TV we would think that only commercial detergents can give a good clean wash. But this is far from the truth. Those special 'lifters' and 'new' or 'improved' formulas are merely marketing gimmicks.

The pioneers strained wood ash through straw to collect lye, which was then mixed with animal fat for heavy duty soap—effective but very drying on the hands.

We've come a long way since then but traditionally laundry soap was always made at home until early last century when it was marketed as a convenient commercial product and the old homemade recipes lost favour.

However, these commercial products were merely a duplicate of homemade products and have never really been improved.

LAUNDRY DETERGENT SUITABLE FOR MACHINES AND HAND WASHING

Mix 1 litre of liquid soap mixture (page 26) with 2 tbsp of washing soda dissolved in 1 cup of water and 1 tbsp of bicarb soda.

Use 1 cup per medium load. Use more for heavily soiled clothes.

If you have hard water add a bit of Borax to soften the water and help get rid of soap residue.

THE COCA-COLA TRICK

Coca-Cola has an amazing number of uses, including degreasing engines as well as cleaning clothes. So if your clothes are very greasy add the contents of a can of Coca-Cola to the wash to dissolve the grease. Flat or fizzy, it makes no difference.

If you aren't a Coca-Cola household then try a ¼ cup of bicarb thrown into the load.

PRE-WASH FORMULA FOR HEAVILY STAINED CLOTHES

Rub the clothes with pure soap and leave to stand overnight.

Or

Dissolve 30ml of washing soda in 2.25L of hot water and rub into the stain before washing (Use rubber gloves to protect your skin as washing soda can burn a bit).

CHEAP NAPPY SOAKERS

Not many people use cloth diapers anymore, it's a shame because it is a far cheaper alternative to disposable diapers and much better for the environment, and they give us an endless supply of soft polishing clothes when the children are toilet trained.

Here's an easy way to keep cloth diapers snowy white. Dissolve 50ml of bicarb soda in a bucket of hot water and soak the diapers overnight. Be sure to put a lid firmly on the bucket, you don't want any inquisitive little people to topple headfirst into the bucket if they decide to explore.

Or

Soak the diapers in some of the liquid soap solution (strong mixture) with some white vinegar or eucalyptus oil, which act as a disinfectant and freshener. Use 250ml of white vinegar or a capful of eucalyptus per bucket.

General soakers for soiled clothes

Bicarb soda is a good soaking agent and removes stains effectively but it doesn't have the full effect of the main ingredient used in commercial soakers—sodium percarbonate (sodium carbonate peroxyhydrate).

Sodium percarbonate is a free flowing powder with a high concentration of available oxygen content offering many of the same functional benefits as liquid hydrogen peroxide, which is not surprising because it is a powdered form of hydrogen peroxide.

It dissolves in water rapidly to release oxygen and is a powerful cleaning, bleaching, stain removing and deodorising agent.

It increases the pH value in washing water. This increased pH value reduces the negative charges of dirt and fibre resulting in strengthening the repellence between the two and making it a powerful stain removing agent.

It boasts the following advantages in laundry formulations:

✦ environmentally friendly
✦ a powerful stain remover
✦ used for deodorising and disinfecting
✦ colour safe and fabric safe
✦ doesn't weaken the strength of fabrics
✦ prevents fabrics from yellowing
✦ effective in a broad range of water temperatures.

As effective as bicarb is as a soaking agent, it's a poor cousin to sodium percarbonate.

It's worth keeping a bag of this magic powder in with your other cleaning agents. It can be bought through selected wholesalers or pool suppliers. It's not cheap but it's a very concentrated agent so you don't need to use much—I look on it as the Rolls Royce of laundry soaking agents. A tiny amount in each soaking bucket works wonders.

TO REMOVE PERSPIRATION STAINS

It's a shame to have good clothes ruined by perspiration stains but don't despair, there are a few simple solutions.

Dissolve 4 tbsp of salt in 1 litre of hot water. Sponge the stained area and keep sponging until the stain disappears.

Or

Try the old shampoo trick to get rid of perspiration or oil stains. Simply rub some shampoo directly onto the stain, leave for a minute or two, rinse and wash as usual. This works well for coloured fabrics, shirt cuffs or collars.

TO REMOVE BLOOD STAINS FROM CLOTHING

Soak the affected clothes in cold salted water then wash in warm soapy water. If the stain persists boil them after they have been washed but this is only for natural fibres that can take a high heat.

Or

Try liquid hydrogen peroxide or sodium percarbonate, both of these work well but read the washing instructions on the label first as some synthetic fabrics may not handle liquid peroxide very well.

If you are using liquid hydrogen peroxide apply it directly to the stain and wash it as you would normally.

If you are using sodium percarbonate, dissolve a very small amount (as little as ¼ or ½ tsp in a litre or two of water) and soak the garment. Sodium percarbonate is a very strong stain remover and you don't need to use much to get a good result.

TO REMOVE MILDEW OR RUST STAINS

Both of these are extremely hard to remove and it's a matter of you win some you lose some. It really depends on the fabric, how long the stain has been there and whether it has been washed or treated before and has 'set'.

Mix some lemon juice and salt together and moisten the stain. Put the garment out into the Sun and get the benefit of the Sun's unique bleaching power. Rinse in clean warm water.

Or

Spread a paste of cream of tartar and water over the area, leave for a few hours then rinse with warm soapy water.

Unfortunately if the stain has 'set' you'll have difficulty removing it but if you can see some change or indication that the stain has faded a bit, it's worth giving the garment a second treatment.

TO STOP GREASE FROM STAINING CLOTHES

If you spill grease on your clothes and can't wash them straight away, sprinkle the affected area with salt to absorb the grease. All you need do then is scrape the grease-soaked salt off your clothes and wash as usual as soon as you have the chance.

TO GET OIL STAINS OUT OF SILK

Have you ever noticed that even the tiniest crumb of food dropped onto a silk shirt seems to spread a wide oil stain? You have to wonder where all the oil came from. But here is a way to fix the problem.

Gently rub some cornflour into the oil stain for a few seconds then very gently brush the cornflour off to get rid of the surface oil. Cover the stain again with more cornflour and let it sit for about an hour or so. By then the cornflour should have soaked up all the oil on the silk.

Shake the garment to get rid of the powder (don't rub it this time, it will spread the stain) and hand wash or if you are a washing machine person, run it through the gentle cycle with a soap suitable for silk.

TO REMOVE WINE STAINS FROM CLOTHING

Ah, the old red wine on the best shirt disaster. No problem.

1. Get a large bowl and put the clothing over the bowl with the stain in the middle.
2. Cover the stain with salt and let it start to soak up the wine then slowly pour boiling water over the area.

Salt is also a good way to soak red wine spills from your carpet. In fact salt will just about soak up anything given the chance.

TO REMOVE LIPSTICK STAINS FROM CLOTHES

If you've had the misfortunate of letting a forgotten tube of lipstick slip through into a wash cycle, you're sure to be more than a bit annoyed at the amazing power the lipstick has of staining virtually every item of clothing in the load. To remove the lipstick, spray the affected area with WD40, rinse and rewash.

STUBBORN STAINS

If you have a stubborn stain on clothing splash some vodka on the stain and rub it for a while, then wash it as usual. A dash of vodka usually does the trick.

SPOT CLEANING

Eucalyptus oil or glycerine removes persistent stains. Place a few drops on the problem area or soak in a solution of half glycerine/half water.

Or

Dissolve 2 tbsp bicarb or washing soda in half a bucket of water and leave clothes to soak for an hour. Wash as usual.

Or

Try lemon juice and white vinegar, they are both good stain removers.

HOME GROWN BLEACH

Lemons are a fantastic bleaching agent, they clean and brighten, have many applications including lightening age spots on skin. One cup of lemon juice in half a bucket of water is an excellent substitute to soaking in bleach.

FABRIC SOFTENER

To make your own fabric softener mix equal quantities of water, bicarb soda and vinegar in a plastic bottle. Don't fill it right to the top because the bicarb and vinegar will fizz up a bit before settling down. Keep at hand and add ¼ cup to your wash.

Or

Washing soda softens the water and keeps clothes soft. If you're using homemade laundry liquid then the washing soda is already in the detergent and your clothes should come off the line soft and fluffy.

If you are machine washing, dissolve ½ cup of washing soda in hot water and use this as an alternative to commercial softener. The amount you need will vary according to the hardness of your water supply.

IRONING FRAGRANCE ENHANCER

The French grannies had a good trick for keeping ladies 'delicates' or 'unmentionables' (as they were called) fresh and delicately perfumed by draping them over a lavender bush to dry in the Sun. This is still a wonderful fabric freshener, it's free and the heat of the Sun releases lavender perfumes that permeate the garments.

Another way of getting the same result without having to display your underwear on a bush is to mix 85ml (give or take) of 90% proof vodka and 12 drops of lavender oil in an airtight container. Let it sit for a day and then add 350ml of water. Give it a good swish around to mix everything together, transfer the mixture to a spray bottle and store in the fridge ready for use. The lavender scent will keep for about six weeks. A fine mist over your 'delicates' will ensure your clothes smell clean and fresh.

EASY SPRAY-ON STARCH

Dissolve 2 tbsp cornstarch in 1 litre of water, put into a spray bottle and shake before each use. Adjust the amount of cornstarch used for lighter or stronger starch and if the nozzle of the spray bottle becomes clogged between uses simply soak in hot water for a few seconds to remove any build-up.

If you want to starch delicate fabrics dissolve a small sachet of gelatine (unflavoured) in 2 cups of hot water, test the solution by trying a corner of the fabric, if the fabric dries sticky it means you have too much gelatine—just add more water to the solution.

SIMPLE HOME SOAKER FOR HANDKERCHIEFS

Not many people use cloth handkerchiefs anymore but for those who do, or live with someone who does, the simple way of getting them clean is to soak them in a salty solution before washing—the salt dissolves the mucous.

TO BRIGHTEN THE COLOUR OF CURTAINS AND RUGS

Check the manufacturer's instructions first before washing. Wash curtains in a strong salt water solution (this brings out the colours in fabrics).

To brighten faded rugs and carpets dip a cloth in a solution of strong salt water, wring it out, wipe over the rug or carpet and you'll be surprised at the result.

ANTI-FREEZE (FOR THOSE WHO LIVE IN COLD CLIMATES)

If you live in a cold climate and can't be bothered with defrosting your laundry after hanging it out to dry, throw a handful of salt in the final rinse and you won't have any problems with rock hard frozen laundry.

TO KEEP FABRICS SMELLING FRESH

There are commercial products on the market that help remove odours from clothes or help freshen up curtains and fabrics that can't be washed often but these products can contain a few nasties including cyclodextrin.

You can make a fabric freshener at home that is just as effective, it kills bacteria (which cause odour) by using vodka, which is basically odourless.

Fill an atomiser and spray as required then hang the garment in a gentle breeze if possible. Always spot check a piece of fabric first.

TO CLEAN YOUR IRON

Try as hard as we can something always seems to melt on the base of the iron making it sticky so it doesn't glide easily. I've even excelled in stupidity by melting the plastic resting tray to the iron. Here's a simple inexpensive trick to keeping the bottom of the iron in good condition.

Put some newspaper on your ironing board, sprinkle it with salt, turn your iron onto a high setting and run the iron over the salt solution to remove the grit.

INDOOR PLANTS TO FRESHEN THE AIR

It's no secret that indoor plants have amazing air purifying quality and their ability to freshen the air, remove toxins and bring beauty to your home is something to embrace.

Plants are so good at filtering air and removing chemicals and toxins that scientists are now experimenting with growing plants along the roadsides that can filter car fumes at an incredible rate—meaning the houses behind busy freeways will have much healthier air. This is the magic of plants!

Many people are put off by the care that indoor plants need but they are incredibly easy to keep alive if you remember to water them. The most common problem is either over watering or underwatering. The easiest way to know what your plant needs is to feel the soil. Just poke your finger in the soil and if it's dry it needs water and if it feels wet it does not! so simple.

A good habit to get into is to check them each week, I do it when I take the wheely bins out, it's just a nice reminder to also check the plants so they don't get forgotten. Then every few months sprinkle some fertiliser capsules around the base of your plant and then leave them to work their magic.

Be warned that indoor house plants can become addictive and once you have seen how much they add to the interior design it's almost impossible to imagine your home without some fresh air makers scattered around. The fact they are also wonderful for your mental health and freshen the air in your home is a bonus.

Easy indoor plants to care for that also freshen your air.

1. **English Ivy:** a lovely plant for hanging baskets that is particularly good at removing secondhand smoke and faecal matter from the air. It is extremely easy to grow and can become invasive so always keep it in pots and trim when necessary. Looks lovely in hanging pots, water once a week and leave it where it can get at least four hours of sunlight a day.

2. **Barberton Daisy:** Bright and colourful and wonderful at detoxing a huge range of toxins found in household materials such as formaldehyde and benzene. Loves a sunny position and moist soil.

3. **Boston Fern:** These are a natural air humidifier, perfect for the bathroom or places that suffer from mould or condensation. These beautiful plants can grow exceptionally large, almost 1.5 metres, so they can really work large areas of your house per plant. They need humid environments, so bathrooms work best or alternatively mist them regularly to keep the leaves from browning. Keep soil moist.

4. **Aloe Vera:** Famous for soothing sunburn, their healing qualities are almost endless! But as easy-care air fresheners these are fabulous for cleaning the air of benzene and formaldehyde that is found in detergents and varnishes.
   These plants are succulents and love sunlight and minimum water, so a windowsill is perfect for them.

5. **Peace Lilly:** These have been popular house plants for the longest time and rightly so, they are beautiful and easy to care for. They can also be divided/propagated over the years giving you more plants as time goes by. These beautiful plants absorb the chemicals from the air and process it in their soil. They are amazingly effective at removing Trichloroethylene, which can be released through paint in furniture. Extremely easy care, leave in a sunny room and water weekly, fertilise if the leaves lose their deep green colour.

6. **Broad Lady Palm:** Brilliant at removing ammonia in the air. These are slow growing but can grow quite large over time. Happy with low light and water only when topsoil is dry.

7. **FIG:** Exceedingly popular house plants and easy to care for if left in the one spot (they do not like to be moved often) excellent at removing toxins like formaldehyde, xylene, and toluene.

These are only a few of the amazing indoor plants you can add to your home to help clean the air of toxins and chemicals. Many annual flowers can also be bought inside to brighten up your room and work their magic!

BATHROOM

We all love a sparkling bathroom. Here are a few recipes that will keep your bathroom glistening and easy to keep clean.

Bathroom tile cleaner

This is a great cleaner but a word of warning first: *never mix ammonia and bleach as it will give off a toxic gas and never breath in ammonia.* Now we've got that out of the way here we go.

½ **cup ammonia**
½ **cup white vinegar**
¼ **cup bicarb soda**
A few drops of citric acid or lemon essential oil (optional)

1. Mix all the ingredients together in a large pouring jar. The bicarb and vinegar will cause a few bubbles so maybe mix it over the sink.
2. Pour the mixture into a spray bottle and fill to the top with warm water.
3. Spray on your shower tiles and leave for 10–15 minutes then wash off with clean warm water. (I use the handheld shower head to rinse the mixture off tiles around the bath.)

Don't be put off by the smell of the vinegar as it will disappear after a while. The vinegar will stop soap scum building up so go with the flow and you'll be rewarded with an easy to clean bathroom.

STAINED OR MOULDY TILES

If your tiles are stained or have mould on them, you can wash them down with a mixture of diluted bleach. A ratio of 1 part bleach to 2 parts water will work. Wipe the tiles with the bleach mixture, leave for 30 minutes then rinse clean with warm water.

Make sure you have washed the bleach off completely before you use the tile cleaner to finish off the job. You don't want any residue of the bleach on the wall to combine with the ammonia of the tile cleaner.

Keeping your glass shower screen clean

Glass shower screens look great but they can be a real problem to keep clean. Soap scum can be caused by minerals in hard water or general household soap. Bars of soap can contain talc and it's either minerals or the talc you see building up on the screen.

Changing from bar soap to liquid soap is one way of reducing soap scum build-up, but for those who like to lather up with a bar of soap here are a few tips.

SIMPLE SPRAY

Spray with pure vinegar and wipe over with a damp cloth. The vinegar will also help to stop new soap scum forming.

Or

Make a mixture of 50% methylated spirits and 50% water. Wipe over with crumpled newspaper. Newspaper leaves an invisible film that stops dirt sticking to the glass.

SHOWER SQUEEGEE

This doesn't stop you ever having to clean the shower screen but it definitely makes it easier.

Leave a window squeegee in the shower recess and train everyone to run the squeegee down the glass before they get out. It will reduce the soap scum build up and your cleaning will be reduced dramatically. It's only a matter of getting everyone into the habit and if you leave the squeegee where they'll virtually have to trip over it to get out there's no excuse.

STUBBORN SOAP SCUM

Sometimes soap scum can be very stubborn—a bit like some people. If you've tried the sprays but find there are some areas of soap build-up that just won't budge use a pad of steel wool (the soaped variety).

Try the lazy man's cleaning method of leaving a mini steel wool pad on the soap tray (in a plastic tray so rust wont stain) for a few days with instructions for everyone having a shower to give the screen a few wipes. Then when the screen is dazzling you with its sparkling clean glass you'll be able to change over to sprays without any problems.

Different soaps and shampoos seem to leave a different residue and if soap scum is left too long it sets hard, almost like concrete. It can be very hard to remove but don't give up because eventually—like all things in life—it has to fall away.

SHOWER SCREEN WIPE

Wipe your shower screen with lavender oil to stop soap scum build up.

KEEPING SHOWER CURTAINS CLEAN

If you use a shower curtain you'll be plagued with the continual build-up of mould, especially along the bottom of the curtain. The easiest way to keep the shower curtain free from mildew is to keep the moisture in the bathroom down to a minimum by making sure the bathroom is aired regularly. Mildew can't form where there is good air circulation.

To prevent mildew forming

To prevent mildew forming soak the curtains in a solution of salted water before you hang them. Make it hard for mildew to get a grip on anything by turning the fan on when you're showering to get as much excess moisture out of the bathroom as possible.

While you're drying yourself leave the shower curtain stretched rather than bunched up at one end of the bath. Put the curtain inside the bath while the excess water runs away then move it to outside the bath where there is better air flow to give the curtain a better chance of drying quickly.

Give the curtain a weekly spray with a weak bleach or vinegar solution or hit it with the Listerine trick to kill mildew spores. Listerine is a great way to get rid of bacteria and other nasties but it needs to be genuine Listerine, the imitation mint mouth washes won't work. Give a light spray, leave for 10–15 minutes then give it a quick scrub and rinse clean.

TO REMOVE MILDEW

If you find the mould build up hard to remove try rubbing bicarb soda before you wash the curtain in hot soapy water and if you hang them straight away the creases will fall out.

I find hand washing much gentler on the curtain than machine washing but if you do throw it into the washing machine make sure you use the delicates cycle.

TO STOP BATHROOM MIRRORS STEAMING UP

Rub the mirror over with a bar of dry soap then polish with a clean cloth. If you do this regularly you won't have any problem with the mirror steaming.

TO REMOVE MINERAL BUILD UP AROUND TAPS

That 'gunk' that you might find on the end of your sink faucet and shower head is most likely caused by what's called *hard water*. Hard water is simply water that has a high mineral content, usually calcium, magnesium, lime or even iron. Although it's not harmful to drink, the mineral content in hard water can adversely affect plumbing and can diminish the effectiveness of soap by producing more soap scum than lather. If you've ever wondered why no matter how much you rinse, you can never eliminate the residue of soap from your hands or shampoo from your hair, or why no matter how regularly you clean them, your shower doors always seem dirty, hard water is the most likely culprit!

It's not easy to get into the crevices around taps and bathroom fittings to get rid of white mineral build up, however if you dampen a cloth with vinegar and wrap the cloth around the tap, leave it overnight and you'll find the mineral deposits will wash away quite easily the next morning.

TO REMOVE MILDEW FROM AROUND SINKS
Make a solution of lemon juice and sea salt and rub it into the area. Leave for 10 minutes then wipe off with a damp cloth.

TO KEEP CEILINGS FREE FROM MILDEW
Spray a mixture of 50% hydrogen peroxide and 50% water on the bathroom ceiling every 6 months to stop mildew forming.

Or

Mix 3 drops of Clove oil in 1 litre of water and use to wipe areas where mildew is prone to develop.

Blocked plug holes and drains
Pour a salt water solution down your drains regularly: ½ cup of salt to 1 litre of hot water is a good ratio. If they are really blocked, wait for them to be completely dry then pour down 1 cup of bicarb soda followed by 1 cup of vinegar. Wait for the fizzing to stop, pour down 1 cup of boiling water. Repeat if necessary.

TO GET RID OF HAIR AND SHAMPOO RESIDUE FROM DRAINS

No-one likes having to pull out the mess that hair and shampoo leave in the bathtub drain. Here's an easy solution. Mix 1 cup of salt with 1 cup of bicarb soda and ½ cup white vinegar, pour down the drain then run the hot tap for a few minutes until the drain is clear.

Gentle bath and tub cleaner

⅓ cup borax
⅓ cup bicarb soda
Your favourite essential oil (optional)

Put everything together in a bowl, making sure the essential oil is mixed through. Sprinkle some of the powder onto a damp scourer and start cleaning, it works wonders. Rinse off with warm water.

Easy to Use Grout Cleaner

Nothing makes the bathroom look shabbier than stained grout. Here's a simple way to fix the problem.

½ cup vinegar
½ cup borax
½ cup bicarb soda

Mix everything together—it should resemble a thick paste. Rub the stained grout with an old toothbrush dipped in the paste then rinse with warm water.

Or

Mix a paste of 2 parts bicarb soda and 2 parts vinegar or lemon juice— it will fizz up a bit. Apply to the grout with a toothbrush, leave for 10 minutes then rinse with warm water.

The toilet (or as it's commonly known—the Throne)

TO CLEAN AND DISINFECT TOILETS

Pour two capfuls of eucalyptus oil down your toilet and 2 tbsp of bicarb soda, leave for a few minutes then scrub with the toilet brush and flush. If you don't have any eucalyptus oil handy you can use vinegar with the same result.

Or

Listerine is another good toilet cleaner. Pour half a capful into the bowl and use a toilet brush to give the bowl a good scrub, wait 15 minutes or so before flushing. Listerine will kill the bacteria, remove stains, and it will also protect the brush at the same time.

It's a good idea to take the toilet seat off every so often, take it outside or put it in the bottom of the shower and give it a good hose down. Most seats come off and slide back on easily. This gives you a chance to get into the underbelly area.

TO REMOVE SCALE FROM THE TOILET BOWL

Pour flat Coca-Cola or Pepsi into the toilet bowl and leave overnight to soak. In the morning give the toilet bowl a good scrub with a firm brush and flush.

Or

Make a paste of borax and lemon juice and apply to the sides of the toilet. Leave for a few hours then scrub the surface with a firm brush and rinse.

CHEAP AIR FRESHENER

Put a few drops of your favourite essential oil on the inside of the toilet roll, where the cardboard tube is. Every time the roll is pulled it will release a pleasant scent.

Or

Light a match and let it burn for a few seconds—this is a quick and effective method.

TO REMOVE ODOURS FROM YOUR BATHROOM

Put a small open container filled with bicarb soda in the corner of the room. Change the bicarb every month or so.

Or

Fill a spray bottle with vinegar and water and keep it handy. Spray to freshen up the room. The vinegar smell will disappear and if you want a lingering smell add your favourite essential oil to the bottle.

TO FRESHEN THE TOILET BRUSH

The toilet brush holder will stay fresh if you keep the brush in good condition. Soak it in a solution of bicarb soda regularly and put a few drops of lemon juice or tea tree oil in the bottom of your toilet brush holder as a double whammy.

PERSONAL CARE

No cleaning book would be complete without a section on cleaning tips to keep ourselves squeaky clean and brimming with the confidence that comes from a healthy, glowing body.

Awesome hand cleaner

To get hands clean after finishing a dirty job use a mixture of sunflower oil mixed with sugar (a small quantity of each is sufficient). Rub the mixture into your hands until they're clean then rinse off with warm water. It keeps well so there's no problem in making up a large quantity and storing in a wide mouth plastic container. Keep near the sink for ease of use.

Quick and easy barrier cream

This is a great cream but it doesn't keep and you'll need to make it as needed. Simply mix an egg yolk with 1–1½ tbsp of sunflower oil and enough kaolin* powder to make a paste. Rub the mixture into your hands before you do any heavy work and it will keep your hands soft and make them easier to clean afterwards.

Koalin (or china clay) will absorb oil and is an excellent cleanser. It also has an astringent effect and is good for removing impurities from your skin. If you have trouble sourcing it locally you can buy it online.

Emergency shaving cream

Need a shave but don't have any shaving cream left? Try using peanut butter; it gives a good shave and leaves the skin soft. This is a suitable recipe for ladies who shave their legs also.

Free liquid soap

Everyone loves a freebie and here's a simple way to keep your liquid soap dispenser constantly full.

Put a container somewhere in the bathroom where you can throw all your leftover bits of soap—the little bits at the end of the bar that are too small to use. Once you have a reasonable amount of scrappy bits grate and combine them with some glycerine and hot water. The hot water will melt everything down to a nice consistency perfect for your soap dispenser.

Teeth

There was a time when it was fashionable to have rotten teeth. Hard to imagine but it's true. Only the wealthy could afford refined food and their recipes called for huge amounts of sugar, which naturally rotted their teeth. Social climbers, impatient for the full rotten teeth look, would blacken their teeth to make sure they fitted into high society.

Around about the same time peasants used sticks as toothbrushes. One end of the stick was carefully separated into long slivers creating what best could be described as a mini broom effect.

We've come a long way and our supermarket shelves are stocked to overflowing with various forms of dental care but there are few that can't be duplicated at home at just a fraction of the cost.

Tooth enamel is 96% minerals and the health of our teeth is dependent on the continual process of the de-mineralising and re-mineralising of the enamel. The trick is to make sure we re-mineralise more than we de-mineralise.

WATER AND TOOTH DECAY

The first line of defence against tooth decay is making sure we have a healthy diet and drink enough water to keep ourselves hydrated. Water is crucial to saliva. Saliva contains calcium and phosphate and acts to cleanse and heal our teeth.

The other way in which water helps prevent tooth decay is as a rinse after you have consumed something acidic (sugary food, soft drinks etc). Rinse then spit the water out and you'll reduce the chances of acid damage, which is the biggest dental problem today.

TOOTHBRUSH

A good toothbrush plays a major role in teeth hygiene and a simple trick to making sure your brush lasts longer is to soak it in salt water before use.

TOOTHPASTE

The role of toothpaste is to remove plaque, keep teeth clean and freshen up the breath. So there are three functions for us to explore.

COMMERCIAL 'LOOK-A-LIKE' TOOTHPASTE

If you like to squeeze your toothpaste from a tube here is a simple and extremely effective homemade product that will leave your teeth so clean and white you'll never be tempted to reach out for the commercial paste again. Simply mix some bicarb soda with a small amount of water to create a paste. Flavour with a few drops of peppermint or spearmint oil.

Or better still, and particularly if you have a problem with an infected tooth, add a drop or two of either clove oil, tea tree extract or olive leaf extract. These three ingredients are superb for infection and the clove oil will take the pain away.

Make your own brand of toothpaste with a little bit of experimentation until you come up with what suits you best. The mixture will dry out after a while so work with small quantities to keep the paste pliable and make sure the lid is kept on the tube when not in use. You can actually buy 'tubes' from health food shops, they're re-useable and easy to fill, or you can cut the end off your commercial toothpaste, fill with your new improved homemade version and seal.

POWDERED TOOTHPASTE

Simply sprinkle bicarb soda on your toothbrush—the taste is rather salty but not unpleasant and if you rinse your mouth afterwards with a solution of water and a few drops of peppermint oil your mouth will be fresh and your teeth plaque free.

If you find sprinkling the powder on the brush too messy then put a small amount of bicarb in the palm of your hand (about the size of a pea) and dip your wet toothbrush into the powder.

DENTURES

If you have false teeth use a solution of bicarb dissolved in water to soak your dentures in to keep them fresh and stain free.

If the dentures are badly stained mix ¼ tsp of citric acid with 1 tsp of bicarb in a glass, pop the dentures in and cover with water. The citric acid and bicarb will bubble and give the dentures a fast and furious clean.

BERRY GOOD TOOTHPASTE

Strawberries and raspberries both make excellent alternatives to toothpaste. Cut the berries in half and rub over the teeth or mash them and use as a paste on your toothbrush. Leave the fruit on your teeth for a while then rinse with clean water. Both berries will prevent tartar build-up and they taste so good.

OIL TO CLEAN TEETH

'Oil pulling' is another effective way to clean your teeth. Swill a teaspoon of olive, sesame or coconut oil around your mouth for a while, about 10–15 minutes before spitting it out. You'll find the oil has changed colour to white and your teeth will feel clean.

Oil pulling has the additional benefit of encouraging saliva and releases minerals back into the mouth, which adds to tooth strength.

TOOTH SOAP

There are a number of commercial products on the market, which can be expensive, but you can substitute the commercial tooth soap for a simple alternative by using a natural, olive oil-based soap. Run your wet brush across the soap until you have enough on the brush to clean your teeth.

Make sure the soap doesn't have any perfumes, unless they are ones you are happy to brush your teeth with, e.g. peppermint.

Using this method is a simple and quick alternative to oil pulling with olive oil.

TEETH WHITENERS

It has become fashionable to have teeth so white people need sunglasses to protect their eyes when you smile but concerns have been raised about the damage some of these processes may cause.

The colour of teeth is determined by extrinsic and intrinsic influences. The extrinsic influences that cause discoloration are poor diet, poor dental hygiene, the use of antibiotics, iron tablets and other substances we put into our mouths.

The intrinsic influences can be genetic or caused by bad dental hygiene. Teeth enamel is a natural pearly white colour over an underlying layer of a yellow hard tissue called dentin. If the enamel is worn away or damaged the yellow of the dentin can show through and if this is the case no amount of whitening of the enamel will change the situation.

If you are looking for a bright pearly white set of teeth here are a few simple, cheap, effective and problem free alternatives. A word of warning, please be careful and protect your precious teeth enamel from damage caused through overzealous hard brushing.

If you are using the bicarb soda homemade toothpaste you already have your teeth whitener built in. Bicarb soda is a superb tooth whitener but if you would like variety here are a few others to consider.

✛ Citrus fruits make an excellent teeth whitener. Mix equal parts of grapefruit, lemon and lime juice and use this on your brush three times a week. Make sure you rinse you mouth thoroughly afterwards because citrus juice is extremely acidic and you're not doing your teeth any favours if you leave acid residue in your mouth for any period of time.

✦ If you have yellow stains on your teeth try brushing with black walnut powder. Black walnut powder will also help remove plaque and tartar but is a bit abrasive, so don't use it too often and be gentle when you brush. Tooth enamel may be hard (in fact it's the hardest substance in our body) but it's also delicate and doesn't take too kindly to rough handling.

TEETH STRENGTHENERS

Have you ever wondered why sugar rots your teeth? The body needs calcium to break sugar down and so pulls calcium from the teeth and wherever else it can get it from (including bones) so the sugar can be processed.

Tooth enamel is only 3mm thick; it's the hardest substance in our body and is in a state of constant mineralization and de-mineralization. Even the smallest changes to the acidity can create weak spots where bacteria can penetrate.

The road to healthy teeth starts when we are very young. Good diet and good dental hygiene practices learned at an early age help our bodies form strong teeth that will last us a lifetime.

Strengthening and protecting teeth is the best way to avoid tooth decay and cavities. Not everyone is fortunate to have strong healthy teeth and here is a simple method for keeping teeth strong and in good condition regardless of your age.

NATURAL STRENGTHENERS FROM NATURE'S CUPBOARD

Include rhubarb in your diet or juice the stalks and use the juice on your brush to protect and strengthen your teeth. Rhubarb has high levels of the mineral salts calcium, potassium and phosphorus, and according to the Eastman Dental Centre in the United Sates, rhubarb juice seems to coat tooth enamel with a protective film.

Another gem from nature's cupboard is the humble date. Dates provide fibre, vitamins, minerals and amino acids but they also provide a rich source of fluorine, and as the name suggests fluorine is a close relative of fluoride but from a natural source. Fluorine helps fight early decay.

MOUTH WASH

This takes a few minutes to make but is well worth the effort.

1. Combine 175ml of water and 60ml of vodka in a saucepan and boil gently for a minute then add 4 tsp of glycerine and 1 tsp of aloe vera gel and simmer for another minute until everything is combined.
2. When the mixture has cooled add 10 or more (to your taste) drops of either peppermint or spearmint oil.
3. Give it a good shake, store in an airtight container and use as needed.

Although there is very little alcohol in the vodka, alcohol does dry the mouth out and can affect the level of saliva so be sure you rinse your mouth with water after use.

BREATH FRESHENERS

Commercial mouth washes and breath fresheners contain a high percentage of alcohol, which dries the mouth and inhibits healthy saliva, as well as glycerine, which coats tooth enamel, blocking re-mineralisation. The best breath freshener is a healthy diet with lots of water but here are a few tricks to keep up your sleeve.

+ Chew parsley to get rid of garlic breath.
+ Make a chewable breath freshener from coffee beans and fresh mint leaves.
+ Chew fennel seeds, they will freshen the mouth (and also inhibit appetite).
+ Eat yoghurt every day—it helps internal bacteria and sweetens the stomach acting as an effective breath freshener.
+ Try a gargle of 1 tsp of honey and 1 tsp of cinnamon powder mixed in hot water, this will keep your mouth fresh throughout the day.

FURRY TONGUE REMEDY

A lot of toothbrushes have a tongue cleaner attachment which can be difficult to use and produces a similar reaction to sticking your finger down your throat. Not a load of fun first thing in the morning.

Furry tongue can be caused by dehydration and rectified by something as simple as making sure your body is hydrated. Although there are other causes including alcohol consumption and smoking, both of which dehydrate the mouth and reduce saliva. If you enjoy the odd drink (or two) or smoke, make sure you drink plenty of water to keep the saliva in your mouth flowing.

Another quick fix is to gargle one teaspoon of bicarb soda in a glass of water three times a week and it won't be long before you see a marked difference.

For those who want to bring in the heavy guns—or for those with a sense of adventure—this is one to have some fun with. Put some bicarb soda on your tongue, making sure it covers the area where the tongue is coated or furry. Before the bicarb has time to absorb saliva (or you are tempted to swallow) add some apple cider vinegar (you don't need much, a tablespoon will do) then close your mouth quickly and swish the mixture around for as long as you are able to hold it while it fizzes and bubbles before spitting out and rinsing your mouth with water. Your mouth (and breath) will stay fresh for hours.

QUICK FIX FOR A FURRY TONGUE

Combine ¼ tsp of citric acid with 1 tsp of bicarb soda—these ingredients are inert while they are in a dry state but leap into life producing a brilliant amount of carbon dioxide bubbles when water is added.

Put ½ tsp of the mixture over your tongue, especially where there is any coating or build-up of bacteria, take a swig from a glass of water, close your mouth and let the bubbles do their magic.

If you find the salty taste unpleasant add a few drops of peppermint to the water for a fresh mint taste.

Deodorants

Your choice of deodorant is very important. The armpit houses a major lymph gland (clears toxins from the body) and it is very important that this lymph gland is not blocked or loaded with aluminium based products, which can cause health problems.

Sweating is our body's natural air-conditioner or cooling system. It's the body's way to regulate body temperature and antiperspirants may not be the best thing to use because they temporarily block the sweat glands and stop them from doing their work. Better a damp patch of perspiration than a blocked lymph gland.

If you would like to make your own chemical free deodorant here are a few suggestions:

+ Use turnip juice—stored in a plastic squirt bottle it is easy to use, won't interfere with the sweat glands and keeps the body fresh for around 10 hours.
+ Try crystal deodorants, they are inexpensive, chemical free and last for ages.
+ Make infusions of the herbs lovage or cleavers, use directly on your underarm or add some to the bath water.
+ Mix cornstarch and bicarb soda together in a ratio of 50-50 and dust your underarms using a powder puff.
+ Try coconut oil. Perspiration is basically water and has no smell—it's bacteria that creates the odour. Extra virgin coconut oil has amazing bacteria killing powers and is also good for skin rashes and cuts, to name a few uses. It's easiest to use when cold (as it solidifies). Simply put a small pea size amount onto your armpit and rub in, as it melts it will turn to oil. My husband swears by this and he works outside all day in the heat. He hasn't used a commercial deodorant for ages and I vouch for the fact that I'm more than happy to get up close and personal to those armpits any time.

HOMEMADE STICK DEODORANT

This is a variation of the cornstarch/bicarb powder deodorant held together with coconut oil. An essential oil fragrance can be added if desired.

Mix cornstarch and bicarb soda in a bowl in equal parts then add a small amount of solid coconut oil. Stir until your mixture reaches a stiff consistency.

Using an empty stick deodorant container or something similar, ram the mixture firmly into the container—keep pushing it in until it is packed tightly. Leave it for a few days to set hard. It should roll on without leaving any film, however in extremely hot weather the coconut oil may liquefy, if it does just move the container to a cool place.

HOMEMADE STICK DEODORANT FOR SENSITIVE SKIN

Prepare as above but increase the cornstarch and decrease the bicarb to a ratio of 60% cornstarch to 40% bicarb. Experiment a bit to see what ratio suits you best.

HOMEMADE DEODORANT SPRAY

Fill a small spray bottle with rubbing alcohol or 95% grain ethyl alcohol and spray underarms to protect against body odour caused by bacteria. A word of friendly advice—this is not a good deodorant to use if you have just shaved your armpits, it will sting a bit.

Shampoo

Our hair is our crowning glory and making your own shampoo is a matter of trial and error because everyone's hair is so different—oily, dry, damaged or coloured. Try some of these recipes and adjust them to suit your personal needs. You may need to develop a few different shampoos to accommodate the quirks of each member of the household but once you get your recipe right, you'll never be tempted to settle for commercial shampoo again.

Most commercial shampoos and conditioners contain sodium laureth sulfate (SLES) and sodium laluryl sulfate (SLS). These are effective foaming agents, known in the industry as surfactants. Both are irritants and cannot be metabolised by the liver, which means they stay in our body tissues for a long time before our body can get rid of them. They are easily absorbed through the skin and once absorbed mimic oestrogen.

They have been linked to a myriad of health problems including female cancers, depleted male fertility, menopausal problems and PMS. It is particularly concerning that it is used in children's bubble bath.

Sodium laureth sulfate and sodium laluryl sulfate are also used in commercial car washers and to degrease engines. Best we avoid both.

Here are a couple of simple shampoo recipes. These homemade products look rather like the commercial ones would look before the sodium laureth sulfate is added and they work just as well for very little or no cost.

A SIMPLE HOMEMADE SHAMPOO

The liquid soap mixture you use for the laundry and kitchen is perfect for hair. Mix in a bit of citric acid or bicarb soda (to help break down grease), wash your hair then rinse with lemon or orange juice diluted in water at a ratio of 1 to 10.

A MILD SHAMPOO FROM THE GARDEN
50g crushed soapwort root
1 litre boiling water

Steep the soapwort root in boiling water for 15 minutes. Strain and use the liquid as a milk shampoo. About half a cup per wash should be adequate.

EGG AND CITRUS SHAMPOO
1 egg yolk
2 tbsp orange or lemon juice*
1 cup of soapwort infusion (as per the recipe for the mild shampoo)

Beat the egg yolk with the citrus juice and add to the soapwort infusion. Use as an all-in-one treatment.

*Lemon juice will give blond highlights. Orange juice is suitable for all hair shades.

DRY SHAMPOO

A quick waterless solution to oily hair between washes is to put some cornflour in a small jar and sprinkle on your hair when needed or use an old make up brush to apply. Add a pinch of cocoa powder if you have dark hair.

Alternately mix equal parts of arrowroot powder with orris root powder, mix well, sprinkle through your hair then rub into the scalp, leave for 10 minutes and brush vigorously to remove the powder. Your hair will look and feel clean and fresh. A great way to keep hair looking good when camping and water is scarce.

SIMPLE DANDRUFF TREATMENT

Dandruff can be a sign that the kidneys are sluggish, try a kidney cleanser or drinking lemon and barley water.

For a simple dandruff treatment make a strong infusion of nettles in a cup of cider vinegar. Use this to massage your scalp twice a day until your scalp is dandruff free.

Or

Rub coconut oil into your scalp, leave for 1 minute then rinse with warm water.

BALDNESS

Having covered recipes for those who have hair let's look at recipes for those who don't have or have very little hair.

Hair follicles are small tubes just below the surface of the scalp that hold the oil glands and hair roots in place. Hair is a protein, which is why good diet and protein is so important for healthy hair. Hair is basically made up of dead cells (keratin, a type of protein) and the only part of the hair that is alive is the root.

Let's cut to the chase and get down to the root of the problem. Baldness, or hair thinning, is a fascinating subject. There some very expensive (and painful) treatments for baldness, however it is possible to reverse some types of baldness with a few simple, inexpensive methods.

There are many reasons for baldness including hereditary, dietary, medications, stress, and even excessive intake of animal fats through over-indulging in fast foods. Another reason for baldness can simply be clogged ducts blocking the growth of new hair, so when the old hair completes its cycle and falls out the new replacement hair is unable to penetrate the blockage. A nice warm steaming poultice could be just the thing to unplug the blockages and get things back to normal.

GARLIC AS A HAIR RESTORER

Crush a clove of garlic to release the juice then gently rub the clove and juice evenly over the scalp. Leave for an hour then add some olive oil to the mix and give your scalp a gentle massage with the emphasis on the word gentle—you don't want to damage any new growth by vigorous rubbing.

Leave the mixture on your scalp overnight then shampoo your hair first thing in the morning. I suggest you use a shower cap to protect your bedding while you sleep.

The heat from your body together with the garlic and olive oil will act as a poultice cleaning the scalp and preparing the way for new hair growth.

Garlic also stimulates the flow of blood (which is reduced through stress and other lifestyle issues), provides nourishment to hair follicles and kills off any germs, parasites or fungi that may be damaging the hair follicles and contributing to the hair loss.

QUICK ONION TREATMENT FOR HAIR RE-GROWTH

Onions have a very high level of sulphur, in fact the highest levels of sulphur in the body are in hair, skin and nails, hence the reason sulphur is called the 'beauty mineral'. Sulphur helps regenerate hair follicles and is also good to promote shiny hair and strong nails.

Juice a raw onion and apply the juice over the scalp, massaging gently so the juice penetrates into the hair roots. Leave the juice on the scalp for around 30 minutes, barely the time it takes to watch the news on TV, then shampoo.

REMOVING CHEWING GUM FROM HAIR
Every parent's nightmare is a combination of hair matted with sticky gum and a whining, wriggling child as you try and pull the gum out. Here's a simple trick to solve the problem. Try rubbing peanut butter on the gum, massage it a bit to work it into the gum and you'll find that you can wipe it off with a cloth.

Pamper packs
These aren't just great treats for yourself; they make brilliant budget savvy gifts as well. Find an old jar and make up a special label as gifts for friends and family, they'll love you for it.

We all hear how bad sugar is for our insides but it's an absolute treat for our skin. It's a perfect scrub base, lasts for months, costs only cents, and it will leave you feeling like you have just left a day spa (where they probably use the same basic ingredients listed in the following recipes). I use sugar to get rid of my 'onion hands' when I have been chopping onions or garlic, it leaves my hands feeling incredible!

HAPPY HANDS SUGAR SCRUB
This recipe came from my little sister who treated us to some of her awesome recipes as Christmas treats.

2½ cups white sugar
1 cup oil (I use olive oil but coconut oil will give you the same results)
2 tbsp lemon juice (or essential oil)
A few pieces of lemon zest (not critical but it gives the mixture a nice fresh smell and helps to get those hands really clean)

1. Mix all the ingredients together then bottle it up and keep it near your sink.

2. To use, wash your hands in warm water then scoop out some hand scrub and scrub away.
3. Rinse in warm water and stand back to admire your freshly smelling, totally clean, silky soft hands.

ELBOW SCRUB WITH VANILLA AND BROWN SUGAR

This one is really good for rough heels and elbows, as an exfoliate for your legs and even as a preparation to remove or prepare for fake tans. It will last for months so there's no problem making up big batches.

2 cups brown sugar

1 cup white sugar

1 cup oil (I use olive oil but if you prefer you can use almond, walnut, sunflower or coconut)

1 tbsp vanilla paste (you can use extract but you won't get the full vanilla impact)

1. Run your fingers through the sugar to remove any lumps then add your oil and the vanilla paste.
2. Mix everything together thoroughly, bottle and seal.
3. To use, simply wet the area you want to treat, apply a small amount of the scrub and massage into your skin in a circular motion.
4. Rinse with warm water, although it's so natural and smells so good you could almost lick it off.

THE ULTIMATE FACIAL SCRUB

This recipe was passed on by a friend and it's a real winner, once tried you'll never be tempted to buy a commercial face scrub again. The recipe uses nature's best rejuvenating products.

Honey is a natural preserver that rehydrates and retains moisture.

Olive oil is another of nature's natural moisturisers. When mixed with lemon juice (a natural bleach for age spots and blemishes) and sugar (a base for the scrub to peel away dead skin cells and open up pores) you have a wonderful healthy scrub for your face, neck and shoulders.

2tbsp honey
1 tbsp lemon juice
1 tbsp olive oil
1½ tbsp white sugar

Mix all ingredients together and store in an airtight container. (The recipe calls for fresh lemon juice so it's best to make up a new batch each week and keep it in the fridge.)

To use: dampen your face with warm water, apply a small amount of the scrub to your fingertips, and rub into the skin using a circular motion over your face, neck and shoulders. Rinse with warm water then stand back and admire the results.

Use twice a week but not more. Scrubs are great for removing dead skin cells but it isn't a case of 'more is better'. If you overuse a scrub there is a chance that you may remove new healthy skin cells as they replace the old spent cells and leave your skin red and irritated.

If you have sensitive skin, try the below recipe without the olive oil and with added bicarb soda.

2 tbsp honey
1½ tbsp lemon juice
1 tbsp bicarb soda
1½ tbsp white sugar

Mix the wet ingredients together. In a separate bowl mix the bicarb and white sugar before adding to the wet ingredients, it will foam a bit as the bicarb hits the lemon juice so make sure you have enough head on the bowl to avoid it spilling over. The foam will go away after a few minutes.

To use: dampen your face with warm water, apply a small amount of the mixture to your fingertips, and rub into the skin using a circular motion over your face, neck and shoulders. Rinse with warm water.

Moisturisers

Now that all the dead cells have been removed and your skin is glowing with healthy radiance it's time to look at moisturisers. Don't reach for overpriced, chemical laden varieties—here are some natural, easy, inexpensive ways to moisturise your skin.

COCONUT OIL

For those of you who haven't had the opportunity to discover the amazing capacity of coconut oil and all its wonders then you are about to be surprised. Coconut oil to the body is what bicarb is to the cupboard—it literally has thousands of uses. You can buy it at any health food shop or local farmer's market and it lasts for months on the shelf, but you have to make sure that you buy the pure 100% coconut oil.

For an easy (and I do mean easy) face moisturiser just apply a small amount of coconut oil to your face and rub in, it may feel greasy but it will be absorbed and leave your skin smooth and hydrated.

Transfer the coconut oil into a handy container for the bathroom, an old pump pack bottle from a previous moisturiser would be ideal.

If straight coconut oil sounds a little too simple to be true don't be fooled—it is one of nature's miracle oils. Coconut oil works wonders for dry and damaged skin, cuts, bruises, and speeds up healing while fighting infection. Coconut oil forms a protective barrier to hold in moisture and also penetrates into the deeper layers of the skin to help keep connective tissues strong and supple.

Coconut oil is readily absorbed into the skin, helping to reduce the appearance of fine lines and wrinkles. It aids in exfoliating the outer layers of dead skin cells, making the skin smoother. Coconut oil is used to treat dry and damaged hair and as a lathering ingredient for natural shampoos and soaps. It also has wonderful antibacterial qualities and can be used as a cream for eczema, rashes and thrush. It's a perfect all-in-one product for men, can be used as a hair gel, shaving cream, deodorant, conditioner, moisturiser and sunburn cream. It will congeal when it cools so you can leave it in the fridge or in your cupboard (it's easier to use when it's cold).

Coconut oil is also fantastic for your insides (and if they are healthy your outsides look much better). There are numerous claims that adding coconut oil to your diet increases energy, balances hormones, and stimulates the thyroid gland. The cholesterol-lowering properties of coconut oil are linked directly to this ability to stimulate thyroid function. Coconut oil raises your metabolic rate, helping to release energy and promote weight loss. Researchers believe that coconut oil is different from other saturated fats because it is composed of medium-chain fatty acids.

Convinced? Hard not to be.

BODY MASK

Try mixing the healing qualities of honey with the hydrating qualities of coconut oil for one of the loveliest body masks imaginable.

Some towels
1 tbsp raw honey
2 tbsp coconut oil
A few drops of your favourite essential oil

1. Mix everything together in a bowl and prepare yourself for a real treat.
2. Wet the towels in warm to hot water and wring out the excess water so the towels are moist but not dripping.
3. Make yourself comfortable, perhaps in the bath or somewhere where you feel relaxed and safe from interruptions.
4. Smear your body with the body mask mixture and cover yourself with the warm moist towels.
5. Let your mind wander and your body relax as you soak up the warmth and healing qualities of this amazing mixture.
6. When the towels are cool it's time to wipe your body clean, removing all traces of the body mask. Your skin will feel as soft as a baby's.

EYE CREAM

No need to buy expensive eye creams, the easiest and most efficient method has been a close kept secret for years. But now the secret's out—simply buy Vitamin E capsules and squeeze a small amount out of a capsule each night.

You don't need much and you'll be surprised at how far a small amount goes. Use a pin to prick a hole in a capsule to avoid wastage.

The skin around the eye is of a finer texture than skin on the rest of your face or body. Vitamin E is the perfect oil for this sensitive area.

SIMPLE FACIAL PAMPER TREATMENT TO EXFOLIATE AND REJUVENATE

Grapes are nature's little balls bouncing with antioxidant packed compounds are a perfect way to rejuvenate your skin.

Use crushed grape seeds to exfoliate your skin and grape juice as a wash to help keep aging skin from sagging. The polyphenols in grape juice keep the skin flexible.

But don't stop there—when you've given your face a good wash over with grape juice don't forget to pamper your whole body by drinking a good sized glassful. New research has shown that the beneficial effects of grapes reduce anti-aging damage caused by sunlight and pollution.

AROMATHERAPY

Please note: many essential oils are highly toxic to animals. Never use or leave essential oils burning around animals. Pure essential oils are very strong and must be used diluted and in moderation. The ideas presented in this section are meant as a supplement, not a substitute, for professional medical care or treatment.

Aromatherapy is a branch of herbal medicine that involves the use of fragrant plant oils called *essential oils* to promote physical and emotional well-being. The use of plant essential oils dates back to ancient times in Egypt, Italy, India and China. French chemist Rene-Maurice Gattefosse coined the term *aromatherapy* in 1937 when he witnessed first-hand the healing power of lavender oil on healing skin burns. Today, aromatherapy is widely practiced and is often integrated into holistic treatments and is used as part of a spa regimen in products such as candles, massage oil, and other relaxation and detoxification materials.

The essential oils used in aromatherapy are *plant volatile oils* from flowers, leaves, stems, buds, branches, or roots that have been extracted using steam distillation, water distillation, cold-pressing (expression), or extraction—which is used on plants too delicate for other methods. The term *volatile* refers to an oil's rapid evaporation rate. Note that essential oils are different from *fixed* or *fatty* oils such as olive oil, which do not evaporate and are consumed for their fatty acids, which provide a multitude of health benefits. And please remember that consumption of undiluted essential oils can be highly toxic.

Essential oils are typically inhaled. They can be used alone or in blends, added to baths, diluted in a carrier oil, or used as massage oils. When inhaled, the scent molecules are thought to travel inside the nose where they stimulate olfactory nerves and eventually parts of the brain that result in a variety of physiological and psychological effects. Essential oils are available in small vials in health food stores, some grocery stores, and online. They can also be found in commercial products such as soaps, lotions, bath salts and candles.

Although it is possible to create your own essential oils with the proper equipment, for the purposes of this book, we will be concentrating on pre-made essential oils that you can incorporate into your housekeeping and wellbeing regimens. I recommend looking into specific titles on the subject of aromatherapy if you would like to try your hand at essential oil extraction.

Widely Used Essential Oils and Herbs

+ **BERGAMOT**
  Primary characteristics: Sweet, fresh, citrus, light, spicy, refreshing, uplifting, calming, soothing.
  Uses: Sore throat, bad breath, flatulence, lack of appetite, cold and flu, anxiety, depression, stress.

+ **BLUE GUM EUCALYPTUS** (Also refer to the section on Eucalyptus on page 36) *Note: Toxic to animals.*
  Primary characteristics: Woodsy, penetrating, fresh, stimulating, clearing, purifying.
  Uses: Burns, blisters, cuts, insect bites, muscle aches, circulation, asthma, bronchitis, cough, sinusitis, cold and flu, headache.

+ CHAMOMILE

Primary characteristics: Fruity, fresh, warm, herbaceous, calming, balancing, relaxing, soothing.

Uses: Inflammation, insect bites, sensitive skin, muscle pain, rheumatism, dyspepsia, menstrual cramps, headache, insomnia, migraine, tension, stress.

+ CINNAMON LEAF

Primary characteristics: Sweet, spicy, peppery, powerful, warming, reviving, strengthening.

Uses: Tooth and gum care, warts, stings, colitis, dyspepsia, cold and flu, stress, nervousness.

+ CLARY SAGE

Primary characteristics: Musky, mellow, sweet, relaxing, balancing, inspiring, revitalising, intoxicating, warming.

Uses: Acne, dandruff, hair loss, oily skin and hair, muscle aches, asthma, cramps, dyspepsia, flatulence, migraine, depression, tension, stress.

+ CLOVE

Primary characteristics: Hot, floral, fruity, peppery, sweet, spicy, stimulating, warming, comforting, purifying, intense.

Uses: Toothache, bruising, cuts, wounds, asthma, bronchitis, dyspepsia, nausea, cold and flu.

+ JASMINE

Primary characteristics: Rich, floral, sweet, exotic, uplifting, balancing, warming.

Uses: Sensitive skin, muscle spasm, cough, depression, stress, nervousness.

✚ LAVENDER

Primary characteristics: Light, floral, mellow, soothing, calming, purifying.

Uses: Acne, allergies, inflammation, insect bites, sunburn, bad breath, nausea, depression, insomnia, stress.

✚ PATCHOULI

Primary characteristics: Fresh, penetrating, woodsy, strong, stimulating, restorative, purifying, reviving, refreshing.

Uses: Hair and scalp conditions, asthma, bronchitis, dyspepsia, flatulence, cold and flu, headache, stress, nervousness.

✚ PEPPERMINT

Primary characteristics: Fresh, bright, clean, restorative, mental stimulant.

Uses: Acne, toothache, sinusitis, cramps, flatulence, nausea, headache, stress, bad breath.

✚ ROSEMARY

Primary characteristics: Fresh, woodsy, strong, stimulating, restorative, reviving, purifying.

Uses: Acne, eczema, hair and scalp, circulation, rheumatism, colitis, dyspepsia, infection, headache, stress, nervousness.

✚ ROSE GERANIUM

Primary characteristics: Floral, fresh, powerful, uplifting, soothing, balancing.

Uses: Acne, burns, cuts, eczema, circulation, menopausal issues, stress, nervousness.

✤ SANDALWOOD

Primary characteristics: Woody, amber, musky, oriental, sensual, masculine, warm, soothing, uplifting, purifying.

Uses: Irritated skin, moisturiser, bronchitis, cough, sore throat, nausea, depression, insomnia, tension, stress.

✤ SPANISH SAGE

Primary characteristics: Fresh, herbaceous, powerful, refreshing, clearing, invigorating.

Uses: Acne, dandruff, hair loss, sores, excessive sweating, arthritis, muscle aches, asthma, cough, cold and flu, headache, stress, nervousness.

✤ SWEET ORANGE

Primary characteristics: Warm, sensual, radiant, fresh, citrus, uplifting, soothing, sedative.

Uses: Dull complexion, obesity, water retention, cold and flu, constipation, dyspepsia, stress, nervousness.

✤ TEA TREE (also refer to section on Tea Tree Oil on page 33)

Note: Highly toxic to animals in all forms including when used in oil burners. Humans should never ingest.

Primary characteristics: Fresh, powerful, pungent, penetrating, stimulating, refreshing.

Uses: Acne, athlete's foot, blisters, burns, bruises, dandruff, insect bites, oily skin, asthma, bronchitis, cough, sinusitis, cold and flu.

BASIC LAVENDER WATER
250ml fresh or 300ml dried lavender flowers
Sheer cloth bag or cheesecloth
Glass container that can withstand boiling water
500ml boiling water
Plastic or glass spray bottle

Place the lavender flowers in the cloth bag or tie them in the cheese-cloth and place the bundle in the glass container. Pour the boiling water over the bundle and cover the container. After the water cools, remove the lavender bundle, squeezing out all the water. Using a clean piece of cheesecloth or a coffee filter, strain the contents of the glass container. Pour the pure lavender water into the spray bottle and store in a cool, dark place.

For Household Use

IRONING WATER

Please note that while some store-bought ironing waters are safe to pour into your iron's steaming element, homemade ironing water is for spraying directly onto the clothing articles to be ironed.

In a sterilised glass bottle with a tight-fitting lid or cap, mix 360ml of purified (distilled) water with 90ml of 90-proof vodka*. Add 10–15 drops of your favourite essential oil or combination of oils. Cap the bottle and shake the mixture well. Let it stand for 24 hours. Pour the ironing water into a spray bottle and you're ready to go. Store it in the refrigerator for future use.

ROOM SPRAY

Making your own air freshening spray is simple. Use small 120ml bottles and keep one in each room of your house containing your favourite scent combination for that room.

Combine 50ml of distilled water with 50ml 90-proof vodka* and 30–40 drops of your chosen essential oil or combination of oils. Shake well and allow the mixture to sit for several hours. This will help the ingredients incorporate. Spray in your room whenever you feel the urge.

*The alcohol in these recipes helps the scent linger for a longer duration.

VAPORISER

Vaporisers (or diffusers or humidifiers) are used to distribute vaporised water and essential oils through the air. The vapour can be inhaled for health purposes such as soothing a cough, clearing phlegm, and calming allergies. Camphor-based additives stimulate nerve endings that relieve the symptoms of pain and itching. Menthol, abundant in peppermint oil, helps to clear the respiratory tract. Rosemary is helpful in treating bronchial asthma. And eucalyptus is widely recognised as a decongestant, expectorant, and room disinfectant.

For Personal Use

HOMEMADE HAND CREAM

In a heavy pot or double boiler, melt together 60ml beeswax and 30ml Shea Butter. When melted, remove the mixture from the heat and add 120ml evening primrose oil and 10 drops of lavender essential oil (or an essential oil of your choosing). Pour the contents into a sterilised jar with a secure lid. Let the mixture harden and the hand softening begin!

FACIAL STEAM BATH

This is a wonderful non-invasive way to unclog your pores. Add 5-15 drops of essential oils to a bowl of hot water. Drape a towel over your head so that the ends hang down below the sides of your face and slightly over your forehead to form a barrier for the steam. Lower your face into the steam, adding an additional one or two drops of oil every five minutes for no more than 15 minutes.

HAIR CARE

Use 8ml of essential oil combined with 500ml of quality shampoo or conditioner as a hair or scalp remedy.

Try:

> Dry hair: cedar wood
>
> Hair loss: juniper, lavender, rosemary or sage
>
> Oily hair: lemongrass or rosemary
>
> Dandruff: tea tree oil

A FEW SUGGESTIONS FOR INHALATION MIXTURES

Combinations of the oils above, along with other essential oils, can produce a variety of aromatic remedies. Follow the instructions on each bottle of essential oil to create the proper dilution of oil in water.

+ **Respiratory health:** Eucalyptus, Lavender, Peppermint
+ **Anti-anxiety:** Bergamot, Clary Sage, Jasmine, Lemon
+ **Irritability:** Sandalwood, Chamomile
+ **Relaxation and sleep:** Lavender and Clary Sage
+ **Insomnia:** Chamomile, Clary Sage, Bergamot
+ **Headache relief:** Peppermint, Lavender, Chamomile
+ **Energising:** Rose Geranium, Rosewood, Rosemary
+ **Relaxation of tissues, muscles and joints:** Lavender, Tangerine, Marjoram, Chamomile
+ **Alertness and mental acuity:** Ginger, Rosemary, Lemon, Peppermint
+ **Stress relief 1:** Cedar, Spruce, Clary Sage, Pine, Ylang Ylang
+ **Stress relief 2:** Clary Sage, Lemon, Lavender
+ **Stress relief 3:** Jasmine, Grapefruit, Ylang Ylang

OUTDOORS

Lots of us love to spend time outside and when the Sun is shining and the day are long — there is nothing better than eating outdoors and moving our living areas outdoors for the sunny seasons.

Here a few tips that we use each summer to make those summertime moments more comfortable and save your garden tools from a short life (or from turning into dry kindling and give your gardening hands awful splinters).

Making your house look like it's been painted for less than $20

There is nothing easier (excluding the elbow grease) to make your house look fresh and clean than giving it a good wash over with sugar soap. The results are quite amazing!

Sugar soap is sold at all hardware shops and supermarkets and has been around forever! And for good reason. Many times before selling a house we gave it a good wash over with sugar soap and water in prep for painting, only to find that the results were so fabulous it didn't need a paint job after all!

Sugar soap is used by diluting in water and all you need is a good bucket and some gloves and a sponge! As it dries it continues to whiten and brighten so the next day your house is even cleaner! (make sure you wear some sort of eye cover to protect your eyes).

Tip: Give your house a wipe down with a cobweb brush (these are a very handy tool to have in your house! They reach extremely high with their retractable pole) and are perfect for sugar soaping hard to reach corners. And they get a wash in the process!

Tip 2: A soft bristled broom with a head small enough to dip into your bucket of sugar soap mix works very well for cleaning up walls without needing a ladder. You can stop the soap from running back down the broom handle (and into your armpits!) by taking a medium sized (10–15cm across) plastic lid from any used container, such as a yoghurt lid, and carefully drilling or cutting a neat hole or cross in the centre so it can be pushed over the broom handle and up towards the broom head, in such a way that it will catch the water running down from the head. Adding some tape or blu tack to seal it tightly around the broom handle finishes the job.

Bugs and insects

MOSQUITO REPELLENT

One of the many problems with the commercial sprays for killing mosquitoes is not only their price but the chemicals we are spraying around the house to add to the cocktail of other chemicals.

Fill a spray bottle with a cheap mouth wash, the el-cheapo from a discount store is perfect. Spray around the doors, windows, the verandah floor or lawn (if you are eating outside), on the chair you are sitting on, in the dog house and anywhere the little blighters are lurking. It will last a few days and give the air a fresh smell. The cost is only a fraction of the commercial chemical sprays and it's safer for you and the environment.

TO RELIEVE THE ITCH OF BITES

When you are bitten by a mosquito only a very small amount of the anti-coagulant chemical (venom) is injected and sits on the top of the bite near the surface of your skin. If you scratch the top of the bite, so that it bleeds, the venom flows out with the blood as the bite bleeds.

If you would prefer not to scratch, dab the spot with some of the mouth wash you have been using as a repellent and the itch will disappear almost immediately.

The degree of itch caused by a mosquito can depend largely on who and what her last victim was, and because a small amount of the previous victim's blood may flow into you as the mosquito sticks her proboscis in through your skin you can sometimes end up with a particularly itchy bite.

If you do experience a very irritating bite try using a mouth wash designed for use when you have a sore throat rather than just the ordinary mint style mouth wash. The mouth wash for sore throats contains a mild anaesthetic that will numb the bite instantly.

Alternatively saltwater or a poultice of salt and olive oil will help relive the itch.

Because mosquitoes can carry disease it's best to avoid being bitten and if bitten attend to the bite as soon as possible.

TO GET RID OF FLEAS IN THE HOME

Flea bites are particularly annoying and you have to feel sorry for the dogs and cats of this world that are infested with fleas. Before fleas become a problem for us they go through many changes, four in fact; egg, larva, pupa and adult. The little black fleas you see, often referred to as ground or sand fleas, are the newly hatched adult flea. They have hatched, unfed, hungry and aggressive. They'll change colour and lighten once they have had their first fill of blood.

Commercial pest treatments are obviously one way but quite often you'll need to have them come back again and again, it can be expensive and if you are trying to go more natural try the simple salt method.

Sprinkle salt over the floors, leave overnight then vacuum. Salt absorbs moisture so it's not a good idea to leave the salt too long before vacuuming because it becomes moist and it's harder to vacuum up.

This salt method is effective on any type of flooring and works by dehydrating the fleas. If you have a particularly bad infestation you can actually see them start to become very agitated and jump around.

After you have vacuumed, empty the contents of your vacuum into a plastic bag, tie the top and dispose of in the outside bin. You may need to repeat the process once or twice. If you see a few of the little black fleas you know another lot have hatched and it's time to dispatch them with the salt treatment.

FIDO THE HOST

A friend of mind tried bathing her dog in salt water after his weekly wash, leaving the solution on him for a while before rinsing him clean. She watched in fascination as the fleas began to abandon Mother-Ship Fido, leaping onto the ground only to die in the salt she had sprinkled around the wash tub. This is a cheap, effective, chemical free and inexpensive solution.

However we don't suggest this for fleas on a cat, we doubt they would appreciate the lingering salty taste which would surely be a deterrent to feline personal hygiene.

LIME AND FLEAS

If you have fleas in the yard the old, and effective, method is to sprinkle lime around the house. This works in the same way as the salt trick and it was by sheer accident (and after long and protracted research) that we discovered lime can negate the effects of commercial pest treatments. We just throw this in to save you from the same learning curve we went through.

STINGS FROM SEA CRITTERS

If you're off to the beach take some meat tenderiser along, the enzymes in the meat tenderiser is a great treatment to relieve stings from jellyfish. Vodka has the same effect so if your day out includes a picnic with a vodka chaser you're doubly protected from the pain of jellyfish stings.

BEE STINGS

Bee stings hurt like hell, more so for the bee because they die as a result of their overenthusiastic attack on your flesh. As soon as you have been bitten cover the area with a generous amount of salt, it will help reduce the pain and swelling. Obviously if you are allergic to bee stings then you'll need urgent medical attention, you don't want to end up in the same state as the bee that stung you!

ANTS

Ants have an amazing and highly developed community culture and they're fascinating to watch but they are also pesky little things if they've decided to move in with you.

Some simple ways to keep them out of the areas where they're determined to go is to draw a chalk line as a barrier or lay down a salt line. Ants hate walking on both and you'll be ant free.

SPIDERS

For those who are terrified of spiders nothing allays the fear of putting a foot into a spider infested boot. Keep the little blighters out by slipping an old stocking over the top of your boots when they're not in use. Make sure you use stockings free from holes and ones that are a nice snug fit.

The same method can be used for shoes left outside for occasional wear, slip them inside stockings and tie the end.

You'll be able to slip your feet into your boots or shoes knowing that there are no nasty little surprises waiting for you.

Outdoor furniture and workspaces

DROP SHEET PILLOWCASES

I use drop sheets for everything (everything except actual drop sheets as I think they are too good for that). One of the best things about drop sheets is that they have a plastic liner on one side. This makes them perfect as gigantic picnic blankets, tablecloths and outdoor pillow covers. You can sew with them like normal fabric and even glue gun them if you do not have a sewing machine. You can also wash them and they last years! I have dyed them to add bright colours and you could add stencil or any sort of artwork to them if you would like.

TO MAKE AN OUTDOOR PILLOWCASE

1. Sit your pillow on the drop sheet and cut the sheet slightly wider than the pillow and 2.5 times longer. Before you remove the pillow, fold the long thin drop sheet over the pillow so that the middle overlaps in the middle of the pillow (this will save you having to add buttons or a zip as it will slip into the case and close itself over).

2. Remove the pillow and turn the sheet plastic side out then pin the sides and sew. This is called an envelope pillowcase and is the easiest to make. It will only take a few minutes on each pillow once you get the hang of it.

3. One you have sewn it, turn it back the right side out (fabric side out and plastic side in) and add your pillow. You now have waterproof cushion covers for your outdoor furniture!

Drop sheets also make fabulous furniture covers. Just drape one over your furniture (inside out) and then pin to shape and fit, sew it and turn back out to have fabric side out and you have lovely natural looking, perfectly fitting, waterproof furniture covers.

Shower curtains are also incredibly useful for outdoor cushion covers or plant covers, they are extremely easy to cut and sew or glue and come in a huge variety of colours and patterns.

WICKER FURNITURE

Wicker furniture tends to dry out when always kept in the Sun and when soaked too often by rain but sometimes you need more than a vacuum to get it clean.

+ To clean very dirty wicker, make a solution of 100ml of wood oil soap and 3L of water. Gently wipe one section of furniture at a time with a wet cloth, using a toothbrush to get at tight spaces in between the weave. Rinse the furniture with a hose and wipe it dry. Allow it to dry completely for 24–48 hours.

+ White wicker tends to yellow with age. To fight the effects of aging, before you store your furniture away for the season, scrub it down with a stiff brush and a saltwater solution of 150g salt and 750ml water. Allow it to completely air dry, preferably in the Sun, before storing.

+ Sprinkle baking soda directly on canvas chairs and hammocks, shaking off the excess, before storing.

+ To get another summer's use out of old, weather-beaten lawn furniture, spruce it up with a baking soda wash. Wipe down all the surfaces with a solution of 50g of baking soda and 1L of water and rinse clean with fresh water.

MOTOR OIL STAINS

To combat motor oil stains in the driveway or sunbathing oil on the deck, pour baking soda liberally on the spot, letting the oil soak in for at least an hour before sweeping the soda away. For a stubborn stain on concrete, try lightly wetting the area before pouring the baking soda on top, let the soda sit for a few minutes before pouring a pot of boiling water on it. Scrub the stain and rinse. Repeat the process if necessary.

REMOVE RUST FROM METAL

Metal fasteners such as bolts, screws, nails, and hinges have a tendency to rust when left outside, exposed to the elements. To remove the rust, place objects in a container and cover with undiluted vinegar. Seal the container, shake it, and let the items soak overnight. The rust should be gone by morning. Make sure to dry the items to prevent corrosion.

OLD PAINTBRUSHES

Old paintbrushes that have dried up can be revived if you've used them with water-based paint. (This won't work with dried-on oil-based paint.) Soak the brushes in a solution of 500ml of hot water,

30ml vinegar and 60ml baking soda. When dry, the bristles should be supple once again.

Cleaning your car

FROST FREE WINDOW CLEANER
Salt reduces the freezing point of water and was used in early versions of refrigeration in 'ice rooms', salt is used to keep highways safe after snow falls and we can use this principle to keep our windows and windshields frost free.

Car windshield: Put some salt in a cloth bag, wet the windshield then wipe it over with the salt bag. It will stop your windshield frosting up in the mornings.

Household windows: You can make the windows in your house frost free by wiping them with a solution of salt water. Alternatively mix vinegar and water in a ratio of 3:1 and spray on the glass as needed.

TO REMOVE DEAD BUGS FROM YOUR CAR
You need to get rid of dead bugs from your car as soon as possible as their guts release acids that will eat into the car's finish. A small squirt of WD40 will loosen the bug so you can hose it off easily. WD40 is a fish-based product and will also remove tar and grime from your car.

To clean the BBQ
Make a paste of equal parts bicarb soda and water. Apply with a wire brush then rinse with warm water and dry.

Alternatively, heat the grill to a high temperature and scrape it with a brass-bristled brush. While it is still hot, fold a paper towel into a tight pad and dip it in olive or vegetable oil. Hold the towel in between tongs and pass it over the grill grate by grate. Replace the paper towel once it becomes too dirty and repeat this process until the towel comes away clean. The grill should have a bright sheen when you're finished.

Occasionally fat from foods drips onto the coals of your fire and causes flare ups. Fight the urge to douse the flames with water, as this is counterproductive—it could send the flares shooting higher and reduce the temperature of the coals. Instead, keep a solution of 500ml of water and 5g baking soda in a spray bottle near your cooking area. Spraying the flames with the baking soda mixture will tame the fire without putting out the coals.

GARDEN TIPS AND TRICKS

A home garden is a source of constant surprise. Nature has an amazing ability to reproduce free of charge to anyone who is willing to tap into her abundant wealth, regardless of whether we have a big or small yard, or even if we have no yard at all! We can all tap into nature's generosity without having to outlay any money.

Friendship gardens seem to have lost favour over the years this is a shame because the idea of sharing cuttings and seeds with friends made a lot of sense and for more than one reason! The plants were adjusted to your climate conditions and you had free expert advice at your fingertips.

Today the trend is to buy established plants from nurseries. We all enjoy browsing through the lush beauty of commercial nurseries however there is a lot we can do to establish our garden free of charge—it will take a little longer, but the savings and enjoyment derived along the way will make it well worth the wait.

Local libraries have some very good books on propagating and the internet has an endless source of information for any plant, tree and flower. If you are keen to start and don't know where, choose a plant that you like and read up on it. Before you know it, you will find new plants and your research will be forever growing and all the while your garden will also be growing.

Some general notes:

+ Lightly sprinkle baking soda on the soil surrounding tomato plants. Not only will it discourage pests from ravaging your plants, but it will produce sweeter tomatoes by lowering their acidity. Tip: Don't discard that box of soda you've been using to deodorise your fridge—it's still effective for use in your garden.

+ If you grow your tomatoes in a container garden, work 5–10ml of baking soda into the soil when you plant your seedlings for the same sweet effect.

+ Occasionally dust a light sprinkle of baking soda around your plant and flower beds to discourage rabbits from having a snack.

+ If you have cracked concrete and sidewalks on your property, prevent grass and weeds from sprouting up by pouring baking soda on the ground and sweeping it into the cracked areas.

+ To clean clay flowerpots without scratching them, avoid scrub brushes and soap. Instead, place a handful of salt on a clean, wet rag and scrub away. Rinse pots well with water.

+ Instead of commercially packaged solutions, add baking soda to the water in your cut flower vase to make the blooms last longer.

Gardening as a hobby

Not many hobbies can bring such joy, exercise, mental clarity and free produce and flowers for your home as gardening can.

Starting with seeds is a great way to go and very satisfying when you see them starting to grow. Start with easy flowers or herbs such as cosmos or chives (seed packets give all the info you need on each packet), grab yourself a bag of seed raising mix and give them a go. Before you know it, you will grow quite attached to your small plants and seedlings and your collection can grow.

Gardening not only adds value to your home (think of the money people pay for landscape gardeners to come in) but also gives you great exercise, exposure to fresh air every day, beautiful fresh produce high in nutrition and vitamins and is also wonderful for your mental health. If you have not tried it definitely give it a go—as far as hobbies go you simply can't beat it.

Growing plants to keep the temperature of your house cool

With climate change affecting us all, much research has gone into natural ways to combat heat effecting homes.

Plants provide an incredible opportunity to cool your home. The difference between houses covered in plants and houses with bricks or timber exposed to the elements is quite dramatic. You can drop the temperature of your house by up to 10 degrees by planting thick hedges around the outside of north-facing external walls (if you're in the southern hemisphere it will be south facing). If you can keep the heat from warming up your house in the first place, you are saving yourself power and cooling bills from using fans and air conditioners.

Make sure to find heat loving plants, give them good water and soil and let nature do the rest—you will also give small creatures a home to live in as well as cool your home.

Easy compost bin

An easy way to get a compost bin is to buy a giant plastic garbage bin, drill some holes along the sides the whole way around so that it has air ventilation and cut a hole in the bottom. Turn it upside down and put it in the area you want to put your compost and simply load up as you need. Use the lid to cover the new opening and bingo a usable easy compost bin!

Whenever you are ready to use your compost you can simply lift the whole bin up and your compost is ready to go.

Just make sure that you always have plenty of airflow and that you put plenty of light material in such as leaves so that you get a good breakdown. If your compost bin starts to get a bit smelly that means it has gone a bit rancid—just add some more lighter materials such as hay, leaves or dry grass and give it a turnover with your garden fork to mix in.

Keeping garden tools clean

Keeping your garden tools stored well will extend their life and keeps plant diseases from spreading. The two tips below are my go-to for keeping everything in one place and its amazingly easy too!

Step 1: Keep a bucket of builders sand mixed with some oil until it has a wet sand consistency (any oil works but for a long life, use oil that won't go rancid such a olive oils) will not only keep rust at bay on your garden tools but also disinfect them so they won't transfer any potential diseases between plants.

Step 2: Simply give your tools a quick spray with metho and water (50/50 ratio works well) then you can stick your tools metal side down in the sand and oil mix to remove the stubborn dirt and keep them rust free for next time.

CANOLA OIL FOR GARDEN TOOLS

This one we use for EVERYTHING! I could say that my husband is a little obsessed with the good old canola oil and there is pretty much nothing left untouched by it in our garden or shed.

I read once that you should not use canola oil on timber etc as it can go rancid. We have never had that problem, in fact, quite the opposite! this may not be the case in a tropical climate—I would love some feedback if you try it. It brings old furniture back to life and soaks in perfectly leaving no smell or sticky residue. The trick is to bake it in the Sun for a while afterwards.

Grab any of your garden rakes, spades, trowels, or anything timber that has been out in the weather and needs some love. Grab an old tin/jar or clean container and an old clean cloth/rag—or even better, a clean paintbrush. Pour some canola oil into the tin and dunk your rag or brush in and then apply moderately to the tools. If it looks like you have gone a little heavy handed, just wipe the excess off with some paper towel and leave to bake in the hot Sun for a few hours. It will give it a new lease of life and make them water resistant and stop splinters forming. It also makes a good film on the metal parts of shovels etc to stop them rusting when not in use.

You can also use canola oil on your outdoor furniture (we have used it on our old dried out garden benches and tables that have been bleached by the Sun). If you have new furniture that has varnish or a waterproof coating over the timber this won't work as the canola won't be able to soak into the wood. Do the same with the furniture as you did with the tools and leave to dry in the hot Sun.

Garden bed ideas

A patch as small as six metres by four metres can provide most of the family's vegetables for a year the best way to start a vegetable patch is just that—start! it doesn't matter whether you know what you're doing, you will learn as you go along. Basically, vegetables need good soil, plenty of sunshine, protection from strong winds and regular watering.

An easy way to start your raised veg bed once it's built is to lay a thick layer of wet cardboard down first then your potting mix or soil, so you do not get grass growing through your soil. There is no need to pull up the grass or use any poison. The soil under your garden will be full of beneficial creatures and bugs and you want them to join your garden not take them away before you start. Also worms LOVE cardboard so you are inviting them to your garden from the get-go—worms are your best friend when it comes to gardens.

Vegetables grown incredibly well in containers so if you are short of space you can start with any vessel that will hold soil, has good drainage and is at least 40cm deep.

Bee boxes are another option to make great instant garden beds. You can find boxes that come as a kit that you put together online and most start at around $14.00 a box. They come in different sizes and heights—make sure that you choose the highest one. Full depth bee boxes these make great instant garden beds just pop them straight onto the grass, line with wet cardboard (make sure to remove all plastic tape before using as these won't break down) then fill with potting mix or soil and plant away! They're brand new treated timber and you can grow anything in them—they also look lovely and decorative.

If you're living in a rental home, building garden beds is not always an option. So, you may need to get creative with temporary garden bed ideas. Something as simple as an old timber bookshelf laid on its side can work very well—fill with soil and plant away, just make sure that there's always good drainage (a good hint is to put gravel on the very bottom layer so that the water will drain out). It may not last as long as a proper treated timber garden bed, but you will still get a couple of good growing seasons out it.

Another great idea that works wonderfully if you have small spaces are styrofoam boxes—you can get these from most fruit shops, supermarkets etc for free! Simply poke some holes in the bottom, add your soil (potting mix and compost from the supermarket will work just fine) and then plant your seedlings straight into it. The styrofoam works as an insulator and the boxes are lovely and deep. You can grow beautiful vegetables such as carrots, basil, lettuce, spinach—the list goes on! You can make a long garden bed along a fence or verandah very well with these and if you don't like the colour of the styrofoam box simply wrap some hessian around it and you will have a beautiful cheap garden bed that could feed a whole family for the whole season. The best part about these is because they are light, you can take them with you if you need to move!

COMPANION PLANTING

Vegetables are like people; you can determine their potential by the company they keep. It is well worth a trip to the library to check out the information on companion planting; some vegetables love each other and thrive when living together, others cannot stand one other and will hold each other back. With a few simple tricks you can increase the yield of some vegetables and this is helpful if space is a problem.

TYRE AND TIER GROWING

Potatoes and tomatoes grow incredibly well in old tyres. You can use them as a portable garden bed or use the tier growing method by adding another tyre to create a deeper growing bed.

Start with one tyre to create a single layer, mix with good soil and some rotting manure and plant your potato seedlings in the soil.

When the plant has grown to around 6 to 7 inches higher than the height of the tire break off the lateral leaves, leaving only the top foliage for the second tier. Add one more tyre to the first and fill with more rich soil, making sure the plan has at least 2 inches of foliage showing. Repeat this one more time, so you have three tires.

When the plants have died off about after three months take the tire apart to harvest.

TOILET ROLLS FOR PLANT POTS OR SEEDLINGS

Keep your toilet paper rolls (the cardboard centre) in a separate bin in your bathroom. It does not take long to get a hefty collection of them and they make fabulous liners or fillers for container plants.

Lay them in the bottom of your planter or container then cover with your soil and compost (make sure to have some gravel or rocks as drainage in the very bottom of your containers) the cardboard breaks down while bulking up your container at the same time. Worms LOVE cardboard and the toilet rolls will attract them through the bottom of your containers as they break down.

CARDBOARD AND GRASS CLIPPINGS FOR
WEED FREE GARDENS

This is an old tip and one I use without fail every year! I swear by this!

Lasagne gardening has been around for ages and is a fabulous way to get your soil in tip top growing condition. But if you are like me and do not have time to make many, many layers and leave them to break down. You can do the cheat's version with cardboard and mower clippings.

Fill your wheelbarrow with water and lay your cardboard boxes (flattened first) in the water. You will need to remove all the sticky tape and plastic from the boxes as they will not break down (your cardboard is food for worms and will total disappear in a matter of months!). Removing the tape when the boxes are saturated with water is much easier than when they are dry.

Dunk your cardboard in the water and push it under (it will only take about 5 minutes to totally saturate each box and you can put a few in at a time). Then lay it over the area you want to supress the weeds.

It's best to weed first (or lay these down before the weeds start to grow in spring). Make sure that you cover ever square centimetre of earth as weeds are determined and will find a way through any gaps! Cover with a good layer of mower clippings from your grass catcher and that's it!

To plant in these beds, simply make a small hole in the mulch mix and plant your seedling. Leave the rest of the mulch untouched to work its magic. This mulch will last up to three months and not only does it add amazing food for your worms, but it also keeps your soil moist and the weeds away! And it is recycling at its best—totally free (boxes can be collected from your local supermarket or cafes for nothing)! And using your mower clippings feeds your soil. I do this each year and am always amazed at how much of difference it makes to the soil in my garden. What was once clay and hard to use soil is now rich and crumbly like chocolate cake!

TIPS:

+ Newspapers will also work but I choose to not use its because of the large amount of ink that breaks down in the soil.
+ The cardboard needs to be fully saturated to work properly and create a seal over the soil. Laying the cardboard then watering will use 10 times more water to get it wet enough to shape over your garden.

+ Make sure all your soil is covered before laying the grass clippings, as any grass that comes in direct contact with the soil will grow grass (lots of seeds in those grass clippings).
+ This works best on soil that has already been weeded but also works on severely overgrown gardens. Just lay a thicker layer of wet cardboard and a heavier layer of clippings to weigh it down or lay some bricks on top to add weight. It will take a lot longer to kill the weeds underneath, but they will add nutrients to the soil, so it is worth the wait.
+ I don't turn my soil over each season, I leave the worms and creatures to work their magic and only plant in the holes that I make through the mulch and cardboard layer, leaving the rest of the garden untouched. This saves so much digging and the soil loves it!
+ Grass clippings generate heat! So, if you live in a hot or dry climate, make sure to rake or move the top layer of grass clippings around regularly (to release the heat) try not to move the cardboard underneath. Water regularly to help it break down or rain will also do the trick.
+ Cardboard will dry and go hard and create a stiff barrier if not watered regularly or kept damp. Make sure to always have it covered so it can break down and not dry out with the Sun.

By the time, your garden is ready for another layer your plants will be big enough to lay the wet cardboard around them. This is a game changer if you do not like weeding or digging!

Free plants and trees

Try simple cuttings to start with—daisies and geraniums are very easy as they strike well and give a wonderful show of flowers.

Climbing geraniums come in a variety of brilliant colours and make great hanging baskets once you get the cuttings up and going—they will provide you and your friends with a source of endless cuttings for future striking.

Poplar oleander trees reproduce very easily from cuttings, you simply stick a cutting in the ground and leave them to do the rest. Once you start growing from cuttings you will soon realise that there is an absolute abundance of plants everywhere! If you carry a pair of snippers in your car and keep your eyes open, you will find unlimited opportunities to collect varieties of all sorts of plants and trees—just remember to never snip from anyone's garden without first asking their permission.

Roadsides and wild gardens are open slather—you may even end up with so many established pots plan you can turn your surplus into cash by selling or swapping.

Herbs also grow beautifully from cuttings. Any Mediterranean plant such as sage, thyme, oregano and rosemary grow beautifully and you can turn one plant into hundreds over the course of a year. Simply find a straight green softwood, trim a 20cm cutting and immediately put it into a plastic bag to retain moisture. Once back home, snip the bottom centimetre off your cutting and gently remove the leaves to halfway up so that you have several leaves on the top and a nice straight stalk of softwood. Pop those in a small plant pot (they work best if placed around the inside edge of the pot). You can fit up to 10 plant cuttings per small pot. Make sure it has good soil with good drainage and that's it!

It can help to put a plastic bag over the pot so that it stays nice and moist (like a mini greenhouse) and very lightly water it regularly. Remember to turn your plastic bag inside out every other day so that you do not get mould growing. By this time next year your one small herb plant could give you 20 or more plants.

You have saved driving to the garden centre, saved plastic packaging and money and learnt a new skill along the way!

Vegetables

Another rewarding pastime is the homegrown vegetable patch.

Since COVID-19 lockdowns around the world, the veggie garden has had a huge resurgence in popularity! Seed merchants have been overwhelmed by the demand for growing your own veg and food.

It's not just great for your physical health but also your mental health. Once again it saves on single use plastic, queuing at supermarkets and gives you the freshest food that is packed with the most minerals as they haven't been sitting in supermarket cold rooms for weeks.

Don't be nervous about starting, just start with something simple like zucchini or tomatoes and expand as you go. It is very addictive so it won't be long before you are growing masses of your own veggies and saving on all those shopping trips to the supermarket—and getting exercise in your garden at the same time!

Veggie garden tips

LETTUCE

Pick the outside leaves of a lettuce as you need them rather than picking the whole plant. The remaining lettuce will continue to grow and one or two lettuce plants should keep you going for months.

Lettuce can go bitter if left too long in the garden, but don't throw it away. Simply rinse the leaves in cold water then dunk in a water bath (deep bowl that will cover all the leaves) that has 2 tbsp sugar and a few ice cubes. Leave for a few minutes then remove and dry on paper towel. Your lettuce will be sweet and crisp.

CAULIFLOWER

Don't pull out the stalk after you have harvested your cauliflower— when left in the ground it will grow leafy side shoots that make an excellent alternative to Brussels sprouts.

CARROTS AND PINEAPPLE

Plant your discarded carrot and pineapple tops—they will reproduce easily from this top section. Pineapples take two years to fruit and will only bear fruit once per plant.

ONIONS

Sprouted onions will grow and reward you with fresh juicy bulbs if you plant them rather than throw them in the compost.

Find the onions that have started to sprout in the bottom of your onion bag or cupboard and simply pop them in some soil, cover up to the green sprouted section and leave to grow. You can continually cut the onion chives off the top and use them in your salads and they will regrow.

FRUIT TREES

Fruit trees produce as much as 30% more fruit if you sink a metre of pipe near the drip line. Put a handful of worms down the pipe, top it up with leaves and compost (particularly pumpkin peel) and this becomes a worm bed that continues to fertilise the tree all year round.

FLOWERING EDIBLE PLANTS

Another great trick to get both colour and edible produce into small spaces is to grow edible flowers. Flowers such as pansies, snapdragons, roses, chives, nasturtium, dandelions and lavender are just a few beautiful plants that provide both colour and food in your garden!

Most herbs will eventually go to flower and they can also be used in flower displays. Add the fact that they not only bring in beneficial insects to your garden and provide colour, but you can add them to your salads, and they are super nutritious.

DON'T DISCARD OLD FLOWERS AND HERBS

If given a chance many flowers and herbs will grow back even if they are only annuals—you may get another season if you leave them in the garden. If you do need to make space and you need to get rid of your old flowers and herbs, pop them in the compost to feed worms or find a small part of your garden or yard and dump all your leftovers and cuttings in this one spot. When spring comes around, you will notice lots of little seedlings popping up and it will save you a trip to the plant store—and also save the plastic pots that seedlings come in. You can simply gently dig your freshly grown seedlings out and replant them in the garden wherever you would like.

SHARING THE GARDENING

If you have a friend that is doing a garden day why not offer your help? Your assistance in return for some cuttings so they are not discarding things that could be used in your garden and vice versa.

ATTRACTING WILDLIFE TO YOUR GARDEN

A garden without wildlife is not really a living garden. Wildlife is one of the wonderful extras that having a garden brings. Children will love it and the little creatures will be grateful for calling your garden home. Many birds, hedgehogs etc will stay with you for years.

By removing any sort of pesticides and sprays you can attract as much wildlife as possible and know they will be happy and safe to munch on the bad bugs and weeds in your garden without worry of poisoning them.

To attract more creatures, leave little water bowls out so things like butterflies and bumblebees can drink. Make sure you put pebbles in there so that they can land and not drown and make sure that you change it regularly so that they have clean water and diseases do not spread.

Stack small piles of sticks in patches of your garden so homes can be made in them. Leave your grass that little bit longer before you mow it, so that the insects can feast on the wildflowers.

Put out bird feeders and bird baths (remember to always use correct bird food and change weekly to stop diseases spreading).

Before you know it your garden will be home to hundreds of interesting creatures and insects. The more plants you have the more wildlife you will get and soon you will have many more families sharing your space and bringing you delight throughout the seasons.

PESTICIDES AND SPRAYS

Pesticides, sprays are other items bought in the supermarket that are wrapped in plastic are non-biodegradable and you really do not need them.

By leaving your garden to happily sort itself out with the good and bad bugs you save money—and your garden will love you for it.

You will be amazed at how elaborate the food chain of garden pests is! By spraying something as simple as spiders or flies you then go on to kill all the little creatures down the line from that. By simply not spraying you bring beneficial insects and creatures into your garden that can enjoy eating your unwanted pests. Before you reach for that can of bug killer, look up a natural alternative, it could be as easy as some dish soap and water!

Garden pest control

Garden pests come in all shapes and sizes, from mould spores to weeds and poisonous plants. Here are some natural remedies to keep your plants healthy and your garden gorgeous.

CABBAGE WORM FIGHTER

Cruciferous vegetables such as broccoli, cauliflower, kale, bok choi, and cabbage (of course) are susceptible to a pest known as the cabbage worm, which is not a worm at all but the larvae of butterflies and moths that use such vegetables as host plants. In the morning or evening, when your plants are wet with dew, dust them with 125g of flour and 150g of salt.

APHID FIGHTER

Aphids (also known as plant lice, greenflies, blackflies, or white-flies) are among the most destructive plant pests. Be a friend to lady bugs (or ladybirds) because they are a naturally occurring threat to aphids. But if you are not lucky enough to have lady bugs living in your garden, make your own safe pesticide. Combine the following ingredients and spray on any leaves where you see aphids. The lemon juice will render the plants inhospitable.

15ml lemon juice
15ml baby shampoo
500ml water

BLACK SPOT FUNGUS/POWDERY MILDEW CONTROL

Roses can easily develop black spot fungus and mildew, which will eventually rid the plant of leaves and can even destroy the flowers if left unchecked. This effect not only makes your rose bushes unattractive but makes it tough for them to survive the winter. Spray the following mixture on leaves once a week early in the morning to keep this nasty disease away.

2L warm water
7g baking soda
2.5ml liquid detergent

POISON IVY KILLER

If you live in North America, it's likely that the mere notion of contacting poison ivy (which isn't ivy at all) makes you shudder and itch. To rid your lawn or wooded area of this rash-causing invader, add 1.5kg of salt to 3.5–4L of soapy water. Spray the leaves and stems of the plant to kill it. If it is covering a particularly large area, go ahead and pour the solution directly onto the plants. Be advised, this mixture will kill all sorts of plants, so take care not to wet anything you want to keep around.

Cleaning your hands

When you work outside, unless you wear gloves, your hands will get dirty and sticky. Here are a couple of effective hand washes for gardeners. Please take care not to use either method if you have cuts and scrapes on your hands or ragged cuticles around your fingernails, the effect will be painful.

GARDENER'S HAND WASH

Apply the technique mentioned above, omitting the soap and simply using equal parts salt and lemon juice. Follow up with hand cream.

PINE TAR REMOVER

It's impossible not to get your hands sticky with pine tar when pruning hedges or hauling a Christmas tree in or out of the house. To remove the fresh-scented stickiness from your hands, forego the turpentine and opt for this natural alternative.

Place about 5g of salt in your hand, followed by a squirt of hand soap and about 5ml of lemon juice. Scrub your hands into a lather until clean. Rinse and follow up with your favourite hand cream as the lemon juice and salt can be abrasive.

THE POWER OF
THE SUN

The power of the Sun has been helping us since the beginning of time for an unlimited number of things, but did you know that it also has so many fabulous cleaning abilities.

When it comes to cleaning, freshening, bleaching, and sanitizing, nothing gets easier than letting the Sun do the work for you.

Did you know that even the famous humanitarian Florence nightingale insisted that hospitals and patients have ample access to sunshine and demanded that all new hospital constructions were built with this in mind, after seeing success with soldiers healing due to the Sun.

So next time it is a perfect sunny day, let the Sun work its magic and save you the elbow grease!

CLEAN WATER FOR PLANTS (AND YOURSELF)

Leaving water out in a glass bottle in the Sun for a few hours will remove the chlorine and purify it. Perfect for your sensitive plants and yourself. Just make sure to remove any lid or covering so that the Sun can penetrate the water and the chlorine in the water can evaporate (and do not drink any water if it has any bugs or debris in it).

SUNSHINE AND BRILLIANT WHITES

Ever wondered why our grannies and nannas always managed such brilliant crisp white sheets and shirts? Some basic laundry detergent (or sunlight soap grated into a pot a boiling water) and the Sun's bleaching power is all that you need. Just remember that any darker coloured fabrics will also bleach if left in the Sun for too long.

NATURAL STAIN REMOVER

If you have an item of clothing or fabric that has a stain that needs removing try spraying the stain with a little vinegar or lemon juice then hanging it in the sunshine for a few hours (only use on white fabric).

FRESHEN YOUR PILLOWS

Pillows can harbour SO many nasties and as they are the closest thing to our faces and our respiratory system each night, giving them some regular sanitising is always a good idea. Any chance you get, remove your pillowcase, and drape your pillows across the clothesline so that both sides can breathe.

If you do not have a clothesline, try leaning them up against a chair and turn them regularly. This not only kills bacteria but also freshens up your pillows and extends their life. Give them a good fluff and shake before you use them. Using the Sun is much better on your lungs than store bought fabric sprays that just mask any odours and leave you breathing in the cleaning chemicals at night.

AIR YOUR MATRESS AND BEDDING

The same as with your pillows, your doonas, heavy blankets and any other bedding needs a good air out and freshen up regularly. If you are lucky enough to have a sunny bedroom, pull back all your blankets each morning and let the Sun bake your sheets. This saves on making the bed and airs out and freshens your bed each day (it can also warm it for you if you get home in time to hop under the covers before the Sun sets). Heavy blankets and doonas can also be draped over the clothesline regularly to sanitise.

HOT WATER BATH

If you have the luxury of a private back yard you can fill an old bathtub outside with fresh water and on a hot summer's day let the Sun heat your water. When you are ready to relax at the end of the day, you can climb into your warm bath and pull a woollen blanket up over the top to keep the heat in and enjoy the long summer nights in comfort.

SMELLY TRAINERS

Simply spray the inside of your trainers with a light misting of slightly diluted vinegar or lemon juice with water and leave in the hot Sun for the day. Remember that it will also bleach them so only try this on white or old sneakers.

FRIDGE TRAYS

Every time you have an empty shelf in your fridge, give it a quick wash in hot soapy dish water and leave outside to dry in the Sun. It will help kill any bacteria in all the nooks and crannies and make cleaning your fridge an easier job when you do get around to it.

WOODEN CHOPPING BOARDS

The best way to disinfect your wooden chopping boards or to remove any onion or garlic smells trapped in them is to give them a good scrub with a scourer in a sink full of very hot soapy water (dish liquid is perfect) then rub half a lemon over them and leave in the Sun to dry completely. Make sure that it is tilted and leaning on something so that the water won't pool and reabsorb into the wood (if you lay it on one side the moisture will get trapped).

TEA TOWELS

Just like chopping boards, tea towels can get musty and smelly over-time. The best way to refresh them is to fill the laundry sink with boiling water (or as hot as you can from the tap) put in three lemons cut into quarters and then add your tea towels and leave to soak for a few hours.

Drain the water, discard the lemons and give the towels a quick ring out with your hands (you could use your washing machine on spin cycle (or pop them in a salad spinner and give them a quick whizz (if you would like to save power) then leave them in the Sun to dry. They will be oil free and fresh and bright white like new! Works wonders on white tablecloths too.

Do not forget anything that comes into contact with lemon juice or too much direct sunlight will cause fading and bleaching so only use on white fabric.

INDEX

Alisa Mayne is the best selling author of several practical books including *Green Stain Busters* and the *Feed Your Family For Less* series. Her experiences growing up self-sufficiently and her 25 years in the food industry, including launching and running many of her own successful food businesses, have led her to share and inspire others with helpful simple life tips, tricks and recipes in an easy and fun way. Her books are aimed to be simple but informative and all are based on real life skills she has learned through the varied and unusual life she has lived. From off-grid farmhouses to inner-city apartments, from Scottish castles to Tropical fruit farms, and from the sunny beaches of Qld to the serene and peaceful small-town life of New Zealand's Deep South, her books encourage readers to give an eco-friendly and budget friendly lifestyle a go.

Cynthia Mayne was considered an expert in the field of budget and natural cooking and cleaning in Australia. Cynthia passed away in 2012 but not before teaching her daughter all she knew from her 40 years of experience.